CAMBRIDGE LIBRARY COLLECTION

Books of enduring scholarly value

History

The books reissued in this series include accounts of historical events and movements by eye-witnesses and contemporaries, as well as landmark studies that assembled significant source materials or developed new historiographical methods. The series includes work in social, political and military history on a wide range of periods and regions, giving modern scholars ready access to influential publications of the past.

Modern Industry in Relation to the Family, Health, Education, Morality

Florence Kelley (1859–1932) was a committed socialist and political reformer who campaigned against child labour in the United States. In 1899 she became the leader of the National Consumers' League, an anti-sweatshop and pro-minimum wage pressure group which she supported until her death. This volume, first published in 1914, describes her views on the problems facing American society due to the expansion of industry. Kelley discusses the negative effects of rapid industrialisation on the American urban working class, in terms of the effects on the family, on the health of workers, on the education of the working class; and discusses the economic 'morality' of controlling the means of production. She also suggests possible legislation to mitigate these problems, some of which later passed into federal law. This volume provides a vivid description of the lives of America's urban working class and illustrates the extent of contemporary industrialisation in America.

T0371371

Cambridge University Press has long been a pioneer in the reissuing of out-of-print titles from its own backlist, producing digital reprints of books that are still sought after by scholars and students but could not be reprinted economically using traditional technology. The Cambridge Library Collection extends this activity to a wider range of books which are still of importance to researchers and professionals, either for the source material they contain, or as landmarks in the history of their academic discipline.

Drawing from the world-renowned collections in the Cambridge University Library, and guided by the advice of experts in each subject area, Cambridge University Press is using state-of-the-art scanning machines in its own Printing House to capture the content of each book selected for inclusion. The files are processed to give a consistently clear, crisp image, and the books finished to the high quality standard for which the Press is recognised around the world. The latest print-on-demand technology ensures that the books will remain available indefinitely, and that orders for single or multiple copies can quickly be supplied.

The Cambridge Library Collection will bring back to life books of enduring scholarly value (including out-of-copyright works originally issued by other publishers) across a wide range of disciplines in the humanities and social sciences and in science and technology.

Modern Industry in Relation to the Family, Health, Education, Morality

FLORENCE KELLEY

CAMBRIDGE UNIVERSITY PRESS

Cambridge, New York, Melbourne, Madrid, Cape Town,
Singapore, São Paolo, Delhi, Tokyo, Mexico City

Published in the United States of America by Cambridge University Press, New York

www.cambridge.org
Information on this title: www.cambridge.org/9781108030205

This edition first published 1914
This digitally printed version 2011

ISBN 978-1-108-03020-5 Paperback

MODERN INDUSTRY

IN RELATION TO
THE FAMILY, HEALTH
EDUCATION, MORALITY

MODERN INDUSTRY

IN RELATION TO
THE FAMILY, HEALTH
EDUCATION, MORALITY

BY

FLORENCE KELLEY

General Secretary, National Consumers' League

LONGMANS, GREEN, AND CO.

FOURTH AVENUE AND 30TH STREET, NEW YORK

LONDON, BOMBAY AND CALCUTTA

1914

NOTE

This volume contains the substance — amplified to accord with the unprecedently rapid progress of legislation — of four lectures given in 1913 at Teachers' College, Columbia University. They formed the opening course of lectures delivered annually under the Isabel Hampton Robb Foundation, established by the National League of Nursing Education.

I

MODERN INDUSTRY IN RELATION TO THE FAMILY

MODERN INDUSTRY AND THE FAMILY

MODERN industry affords, in more generous measure than the human race has before known them, all those goods which form the material basis of family life—food, clothing, shelter, and the materials and opportunities for subsistence for husband, wife and children.

But modern industry tends to disintegrate the family, so threatens it that the civilized nations are, and for at least one generation have been, actively building a code intended to save the family from this destructive pressure.

This is the paradox of Modern Industry.

It is my object to illustrate this paradox by indicating some forms of the pressure of industry upon the family, and upon each of its elements.

The American ideal of the home—inherited from the time when we were an agricultural country—includes father, mother and children living together in a house; the father the breadwinner, the mother the homemaker, the children at play and at school until they reach a reasonable age for work—the boys helping their fathers with the chores, and the girls learning under their mothers' eyes the arts of the housewife, the house which shelters this group being the property of the family or in process of becoming their property. Originally, the typical home was a farm which furnished subsistence, and the children received within the family group industrial, religious and moral training. Our departure from this early ideal under the pressure of modern industry is conspicuous.

The paradoxical tendency of the family to disintegrate under pressure of the same industry which affords it infinite material enrichment offers the key to a complex, varied legislative movement going forward in all the civilized nations. Seemingly incoherent, this movement is a ramified effort to safeguard the family. The mind is wearied even by a partial enumeration of the elements of the industrial and political code upon which the modern world is at work to this end.*

* Among those elements the following are important:

a. Compulsory arbitration of labor disputes;

b. Workmen's compensation and social insurance, factory inspection and compulsory provision of fire precautions and safety devices;

c. Regulation of working time, including one day's rest in seven, a short working day, prohibition of night work for

Such effort to bulwark the family by comprehensive legislation arises because, all over the modern world, a large and increasing proportion of husbands and fathers are by the nature of their work taken out of their homes, or killed outright, or maimed, or they are disabled by industrial diseases, and thus disqualified for their normal duty of breadwinner.

Or throughout long periods of seasonal unemployment they are recurrently without earnings. Even when in health and at work, unskilled laborers and many employees of higher grade are so far underpaid that they cannot maintain their wives and children, who are, therefore, drawn out of the home into industry to supplement the earnings of the father; or the home is invaded under the sweating system by the materials of industry.

women and children, and the utmost attainable restriction of night work for men;

d. Prohibition of child labor and of homework under the sweating system;

e. Minimum wage boards and widows' pensions with generous provision for institutional care of certain classes of diseased and defective children;

f. Compulsory education prolonged for part time instruction throughout minority;

g. Housing codes;

h. Pure food laws;

i. The enfranchisement of women.

Tendency to Celibacy

Vast numbers of men never found families at all, because they fear to marry upon insufficient wages insecurely held by reason of the precarious nature of many employments; or because their health is destroyed before they reach an economic position which seems to them to justify marriage; or because the girls whom they would gladly marry are worn out and broken down in the service of industry.

Abjuring family life is a social loss from every point of view, most of all when the men who thus deny themselves are of a high type and animated by unselfishness. Citizens of Cincinnati are erecting a memorial to such a man, Joe Haeberle, once head of the truck drivers' union of that city. This self-taught German immigrant worked himself literally to death in the service of the children of Ohio. Having obtained some drinking fountains for the teamsters' horses, he discovered that the children made them centres of their play during school hours. Thus he learned that great numbers of children were out of school because Cincinnati had not, at that time, free school books. For many years he carried on the agitation for free books, for effective compulsory education and, at the last, for workable child labor laws. Hampered by his foreign accent, his uncouth, ill-fitting clothes, and his uncertain teamster's gait, Joe Haeberle spent every free evening, every holiday, every Sunday struggling against indifference, and prejudice, and active, open hostility, to get for the children of Ohio the best that any state gives its children. A few months before his too early death, he told one of his friends that he had never been willing to ask a woman to share with him the hardships of life on the only earnings he could hope for, ten dollars a week. Faithful to his ideal of the society of the future in which all children should have the opportunity of education, unselfish in his life and his death, this tender, devoted servant of the children lived and died wifeless and childless.

Compulsory celibacy is the lot of vast numbers of men employed upon reclamation schemes, building railways, tunnels and water power constructions. Sometimes the work lies far from civilization, but oftener—as in Massachusetts, Connecticut and New York—the inhumane arrangements of the construction companies and contractors make family life impossible for men who do this work. Worn-out freight cars and vermin-ridden bunk houses are not fit homes for wives and children. But these are the dwellings afforded for rapidly increasing thousands of work-

ing men, for years at a time, a group being moved
from one section to another of some great undertaking, the quality of their quarters varying little.

Of all the occupations which detach men from
home life the oldest is that of the sailors. In
Phœnicia, in the Greece of Homer, their craft
was already an ancient one. In our ports as then
the sailors are proverbially homeless, and their
numbers grow as the industry of Europe, particularly that of Germany and England, lives increasingly by manufacturing and distributing throughout the world raw materials from the Tropics,
these nations importing meanwhile in ever larger
proportion their own food supplies.*

New and characteristic of modern industry is
the myriad of men who float about on land, their
family life reduced to a minimum by the nature
of their occupations, among whom are commercial travellers, kept perforce away from their families a large part of every year. Sleeping car conductors and porters, and dining car waiters, leaving New York to go to Chicago, may there find orders to go on to Seattle or San Diego, and do not
know when they will again reach home. In general, family life in the home is obviously mini-
mized for all those husbands and fathers whose

* The phenomenal development of the cocoa and chocolate
industry and of rubber production are cases in point.

work keeps them travelling, e. g., railway engineers, firemen and brakemen, conductors, porters and waiters.

Hotel employés, cooks and waiters, and domestic servants are virtually condemned by the present organization of their occupations to separation from their wives and children. And the demand of the last named employment for surrender of the family tie is obviously an element in the permanent, universal, unorganized boycott of domestic service by American men. Native white American valets, footmen and butlers virtually do not exist.

When the farm gave us our ideal of family life, many varieties of industrial activity were carried on upon farms and in rural villages. The village blacksmith once made the plough which the farmer owned. Now the city of Moline has grown up around the plough-making industry, producing millions of ploughs. South Bend makes agricultural wagons, and Auburn manufactures the farmers' binding twine. Many cities thus specialize, each in one industry formerly conducted on the farms.

While those industries have gone from rural life, a new disintegrating element has arisen in the floating agricultural workers, a new apparition from the city invading the country for a part of the year. When a Settlement recently wished to send a young man to work on a Connecticut farm, some forty farmers replied that there would be work not for the whole year, but for a few months only. For the prospective farm laborer in a New England state these offers meant the choice over the winter between tramping and the city lodging house.

In the West thousands of men now go annually from the cities to work in the grain harvest for a period varying from five to nine months. At Hull House, years ago, it was horrifying to discover, in the neighboring frame cottages, Italian women with children living four families in four rooms of a flat, one wife and her children in one room, because the four men breadwinners of the families had gone, early in the spring, to work on the railroads. Later the men would leave the railroads for the harvesting, beginning in Texas or Arkansas, working northward into Western Canada, and returning home to Chicago toward Thanksgiving. Sometimes they did not come back at all. After the harvest every year, families were left fatherless by this new American agriculture. We thought of this development of pressure of industry upon family life as an episode.

After twenty years we know, however, that it

is a regular part of Western American agriculture, which affords no foundation for normal home life for these thousands of migratory employés. In the canning industry there are, besides floating families of workers in buildings and sheds, vegetable and berry pickers by thousands of families in fields. That is one most striking change that modern industry has wrought in agriculture and its immediate derivative industries, canning and fruit preserving. In the West it is men who migrate in the service of agriculture. In the East it is largely women with numerous young children.

In the case of sailors, the nature of the work itself involves the sacrifice of family life in the home. In many other industries, however, the sacrifice is wantonly exacted, as when city railway companies require the twelve hours day, and the seven days week, and their men are never at home to see the children awake. The federal statute intended to preserve the health of railway employés in interstate commerce permits them to work sixteen hours in twenty-four!

Night work done in paper mills, glassworks, and steel manufacture, and a growing number of continuous industries keeps fathers away from home and makes impossible any wholesome domestic companionship. A father at home by day, who is trying to make up sleep lost the night before while at work, is not a helpful element of the family life.

Night work of many kinds is obviously unavoidable. Its present rapidly increasing dislocation of family life is, however, doubtless destined to be checked in proportion as the workers attain a deciding voice by strengthening their labor organizations, or by using their votes more wisely, or even by convincing the courts that the present distribution of working hours is contrary to sound public policy.

In the interest of the family life of wage earners, to assure to fathers opportunity of companionship with their wives and children, we Americans, in the Twentieth Century, have to strive to get by statute that which was laid upon the race by the Commandments, namely, one day's rest in seven. This was commanded as of equal importance with the injunction, Thou Shalt Not Kill. The Book of Genesis records that the Lord rested upon the seventh day.

Destruction of Fathers and Injury of Mothers

When families are founded they are, with appalling frequency, disrupted by the destruction that industry entails upon breadwinners. In New York, this greatest of all the industrial states, our highest court has held within three years that, to compel employers to pay a fixed compensation to injured employés or surviving widows and children, would be taking property from the employers without due process of law. Yet the process provided by the statute embodied the principles common to the compensation laws of modern industrial nations.* Workmen's compensation was thus held contrary to our constitution. Until this decision can be reversed, working people will have, in this state, only the barest gambling chance to receive, under the common law, some quite incalculable sum awarded by a jury, after years of delay in the courts. And the most dynamic of all stimuli—the financial incentive for making industry safe—is withdrawn from employers.

Under this decision industry does not pay its bills in the greatest industrial state in the Republic. If a railroad has killed the breadwinner of a

* Ives case, Court of Appeals of New York, March 24, 1911. Judge Werner, the presiding judge of the New York Court of Appeals, who wrote the decision in the Ives case, was not re-elected to succeed himself at the election in November, 1913. At the same election the New York State Constitution was amended by a popular vote for the purpose of facilitating legislation creating workmen's compensation. In December, 1913, a statute was enacted in accordance with the powers conferred by the amended Constitution. This new statute also will, however, be tested as to its constitutionality in due time by the New York Court of Appeals.

family, the railroad industry is not now legally
the debtor of his widow during widowhood, and
of the fatherless children even until the 16th
birthday. If the breadwinner is not killed but
disabled by an injury incident to his work, or by
an industrial disease, transforming him from the
breadwinner to a dragging burden upon his wife
and children, they need not less but greater in-
demnification for their loss, not from taxes, or
charity, but from the industry which deprives
them of their breadwinner. We are, as a nation,
far slower than the nations of Europe to enforce
the payment of this debt to families bereft by industry of their breadwinners.*

As marriages fail to occur, and families fail to
be founded, because of fear of poverty, so, also, in
many families children are not born, or come into
life cruelly handicapped, because of the effects of
industry upon the health of the mothers while, as
young girls and young women, they worked for
wages.   Sterility among working class wives,
caused by protracted standing while at work in
their girlhood, is a source of apprehension among
physicians whose practice brings wage-earning
women patients under observation.   Sir Thomas

* Obviously, the final simplification of the vexed problem
of widows' pensions lies in the direction of keeping fathers
alive, in good health and at work.

Oliver, the learned and sympathetic English student of American industry from the medical point of view, recently published, after a journey among American factories, a warning as to the effect on the future of the Republic of the employment of so many young women in manufacture.

The absence from home at night of thousands of young girls in the telephone service has become a matter of course. Seventy-five per cent. of these young workers at night are at the age of 18 years, according to the latest official report of this state. Sleep lost at night cannot be made up by day by people who live in the industrial districts of any city. What nation ever before took it for granted that thousands of young girls 18 years old should, in the way of earning their bread, be away from home at night? This employment of young girls may well be taken as an index of cynicism of public opinion which accepts, under the corrupting influence of industry, such disintegration of the family as inevitable.

The field of employment constantly widens in which wives are expected to earn wages, as in tobacco factories, laundries, cigar making, the garment trades, and the textiles. It is no longer especially characteristic of any part of the country (as the cotton mill regions of New England) or of any one industry (as the textiles) that women continue wage earning after marriage. The custom tends to become universal. Industry now counts upon having not only men and girls—as was for some generations characteristic of American manufacture—but married women as well. Girls marry with the knowledge that as wives they will have to work for wages, and accept it as the will of God, or the course of Nature, when in their families babies die.

Family life in the home is sapped in its foundations when the mothers of young children work for wages. Yet each Census shows a greater number of cities where married women are so employed and infant mortality ranges high. In Fall River, the characteristic textile manufacturing city of New England, not only is the general death rate higher than in any other city of the same size, but infant mortality in particular reaches an appalling figure.* This has been the history of the textile industries wherever they have been developed—in Germany, in England, in this country—a high infant death rate has been their by-product. The double task laid upon mothers in such industrial communities is more than they can perform, and the babies pay the penalty with their lives.

*Census of 1910, and Federal Report on the Conditions of Labor of Woman and Child Wage-Earners.

The fact is moreover increasingly conspicuous that, in working class districts of manufacturing cities, the death rate of infants is far in excess of that in regions inhabited by prosperous people in the same cities. The children are consumed, directly or indirectly, in the process of producing goods, and this while they are within the closest embrace of the family, before they are old enough for the kindergarten.

Throughout all civilization wages in industries which employ married women tend to range so low that only when the whole family is drawn into wage earning can a subsistence be earned. In this country it is relatively new, but here, as elsewhere, when the textile industries develop, this disintegration proceeds conspicuously. Except that men in the occupation are largely supplanted by their own wives and children, it might truthfully be said that the family is bodily transferred from the home to the mill.

When wives are engaged in night work, the effect is devastating. Yet in the cotton mills of the southern states such work is not exceptional, it is a commonplace part of the life of many mill communities.

Withdrawal of Children from Homes

In most industrially developed states the community says to the parent: "You may not let your child work (except as a newsboy) before its 14th birthday. You must keep your child in school at least until that birthday, and beyond it unless the child meets certain fixed requirements as to stature, health and ability to read and write English. You must, moreover, feed and clothe your boy or girl according to a minimum set for you by usage. Failing in these things, appropriate penalties await you, among which is sheer deprivation of the guardianship of your child."

In New York State 38,000 children are maintained in institutions, paid for out of taxes, because their natural guardians fail to meet these requirements. Few of these institutions are schools in any true sense. Fewer still are colonies for the care of afflicted children for whom segregation is needed—the mentally deficient, or advanced cases of tuberculosis. In the main they are free municipal boarding houses, communist institutions in which various religious sects attempt the task, financed out of taxes, of bringing up children by wholesale. Undesirable though it is, this undertaking constitutes at present the sole official attempt of state or city to eke out the efforts of parents who fail, under the pressure of industry, to meet modern requirements.

Institutional care is, however, an attempt to substitute charity for justice, necessary so long as industry does not pay its debts to the disabled and the bereft.

The stern pressure upon parents has led to a nation-wide agitation for public pensions for widows, mothers' pensions or "funds to parents" acts. And states, cities and charitable organizations now vie with each other in assuring us that no child need be undernourished, or unfitted for school life by reason of destitution.*

Even more numerous than the families whose breadwinners are dead or disabled are those whose able-bodied fathers, working in underpaid industries for an insufficient annual income, cannot support the children as the community demands. These account, perhaps more than all other influences combined for the exodus from home to mill and mine of boys and girls who should still be school children.

There is a tremendous and growing draft of children out of the home into industry. In 1912 in New York City alone 42,000 children, boys and

* The change of attitude on this subject in the brief period since the appearance of Robert Hunter's volume on Poverty is striking.

girls below the age of 16 years, were given working papers. In all history this is new. Never before this modern industrial era did tens of thousands of young girls and boys in a single city enter upon industry away from all control by parents or by responsible masters under some form of regulated indenture. Regularly each year, in this city alone, more than forty thousand boys and girls enter as independent units into the world of labor.

The law authorizes the father and mother to collect wages of minor children. But the employer has no responsibility for getting the wage into the hands of parents. Nor is there any responsibility upon employers for the health and morals of these young workers. No one who has not lived long in the foreign colonies can estimate what it means to an immigrant parent, when a boy decides that he will no longer acknowledge a duty to his parents and brothers and sisters, will no longer carry home his wages. In serving on a scholarship committee it is startling to read in the family record that there are two older brothers or two older sisters, who recognize no duty toward their parents or the younger child—the candidate for a scholarship—who is left to suffer hardship or to accept charity. We acquiesce very generally in the loss of the sense of duty toward the family on the part of sons and daughters because industry has habituated us, and tempted them, to consider the worker as an isolated unit, regardless of family ties.

The House as the Home

Our traditional national ideal of family life includes owning a home, or entering upon the task of acquiring one.

Modern industry achieves for business uses the forty stories of the Metropolitan Tower and the fifty floors of the Woolworth Building, cheering the eyes of the city with their beauty. But for the homes of families who work there is maintained—and urgently needed—a nationwide crusade for a minimum standard of construction. Philanthropy is not yet nobly striving to establish among working people lofty ideals of healthfulness, beauty and comfort, in homes wherein a worthy life may be lived and childhood may spend its years in care-free play. Far from it, we are still amply occupied in striving through philanthropic effort and penal statutes to establish *minimum* standards below which none may descend.

In one-room log cabins among cotton fields in Georgia and the Carolinas, in fifty-family tenements in New York City, and in the repellent shacks of miners' families in a dozen mining states, the irony is the same. Families who work are so ill housed that it is a problem of self-defence for civilization to set a lowest level beneath which no southern plantation owner, no mining company, no jerry-building city landlord may offer so-called "homes."

Recently I had occasion to come up from Jacksonville, Florida, through Georgia, the Carolinas, and part of Virginia by day. Every new cotton mill along the railway is costlier, more modern, and better equipped than the last. But nothing could be more discouraging than the monotonous homes surrounding those mills. We have no dignified ideal of family homes for wage-earning families. The farm houses of an older generation, owned by their occupants, austere in their simplicity, had at least a certain dignity. It is appalling that American people who leave the farms acquiesce in living in the homes provided for them in the industrial centres by the industry of to-day.

Everywhere, the world over, those who would build wholesome and beautiful houses for working families, and keep them free from invasion by industry, are confronted by an insoluble problem. Everywhere this problem consists of the same two factors—the low family income of laborers, and the monopoly power of landowners to make their own terms for selling, leasing, renting land for homes.

In New York and Chicago, in congested districts where overcrowding is a perennial source of disease, I have for more than 20 years observed the landlords resisting every attempt to raise the standard of workmen's city dwellings. In New York, after generations of tenement house reform, the number of sunless rooms constantly increases. Every new tenement is larger, built to shelter more people than the house which it displaces. Infants and young children—the tenderest, most perishable members of the family—succumb most quickly to the enfeebling influence of sunless dwellings, overcrowding and bad air. And the survivors carry with them through life the effects upon body and character of this bad beginning. Overcrowding and decency are mutually exclusive.

Overcrowding in tenements arises in part from the fact that, among unskilled workers, the small and irregular family wage compels the choice to be made between food and rent. The question forever confronting the unskilled laborer's family is: "Shall we have more food and less space?" If the decision is in favor of more food, a lodger or boarder is commonly added to the already large number of occupants of the flat, with all the demoralization and danger arising from the presence

of an outsider, a non-member of the family.   A
neighbor of mine, a tailor out of work, took in a
man who shared the bed of the youngest son. The
little boy acquired, after a single night, an infec-
tion which left him hopelessly, incurably blind.

These facts are all well known, the story of the
tenements and their dwellers has long been thread-
bare, the effort to deal with them has long been
a weariness to the flesh. The tenements persist
and increase from generation to generation. This
is precisely the reason for presenting them once
more—this sinister circumstance that, in spite of
the teachings of modern science and the efforts
to apply modern hygiene to every relation of life,
overcrowded tenements are still here, and New
York City still suffers, in the Borough of Man-
hattan, the densest congestion of population in
the history of the world. And this in spite of all
the wealth created by modern industry.

The explanation is to be found in the control
of industry itself over the minds of reformers
and of the authorities.   It is, indeed, industry
which calls people to the congested centres by its
offer of varied work.* It is the Allied Real Estate
industry, the brokers, the builders, the speculators
in land and shelter, who constitute the active

* We have no coherent policy, in any state, calculated to
draw population away from congested city districts.

enemy to housing progress, just as it is manufacturing industry which calls little girls from school to factory, and commercial industry which sells foul milk to be fed to babies.

To deal with modern real estate industry in this unlovely rôle of obstacle to progress we have had, hitherto, only little groups of reformers applying little remedies. And the continuance of the evil witnesses our failure.

Alone in all the world, our reformers discuss houses as though they were balloons, or biplanes, or clouds floating aloft unrelated to the land on which they stand, unaffected by taxation, detached from the whole plan of the city of which they form so essential and injurious a part. For generations our reformers have continued to do this, untaught by failure, unstirred by the experiments of other cities in other lands.

The comprehensive national policy of Australia and New Zealand, applied to distributing population, is too well known and too elaborate to be summarized within the limits of a lecture. In our neighboring country, Canada, Vancouver has untaxed all buildings by way of placing a premium upon constructing more of them. England exhibits—besides all the changes arising from the Lloyd-George land taxes—encouraging experiments in the Garden Cities, in corporate ownership of land for the common good of the inhabitants. Port Sunlight and Bournemouth are familiar examples and others, less well known, are growing up in many parts of England. In Germany, Frankfort· and Ulm have for a quarter century been acquiring land, in their municipal capacity, for the express purpose of housing working people in homes satisfactory to them.

We, meanwhile, still putter along with prohibitions and regulations upon owners, builders, speculators whom we accept as inevitable. We seem unteachable, refractory to enlightenment drawn from our own experience of failure, or from the stimulating examples to be found in other lands.

Why have we no permanent Federal Commission on Homes?

Invasion of the Home by Manufacture

In New York City, the greatest, richest centre of modern industry in the Western Hemisphere, the home, the house, the tenement—far from sheltering the family and belonging to it, consumes the family. The tenement house is proverbially a breeding place of tuberculosis and other social diseases. The high cost of land leads to congestion of buildings, and this in turn to insufficient light, air and space for the family dwelling. To earn a share of the rent for cramped, unwholesome quarters, mothers are withdrawn from household work, and children stay from school. They are drawn into industry, and the kitchen and bedroom become their workplaces.

The assumption universally underlies women's wages that there is always a male breadwinner successfully performing his allotted task, and any earnings of wife and daughter are pin money added to his steady income. In fact, however, in the chaos of modern industry, the male adult breadwinner—father or older brother—happens with tragic frequency to be dead, killed outright perhaps by his work—a railway accident, a Titanic disaster, a mine collapse. Or he may be gradually poisoned by the materials of his work, or exhausted by its processes. He may be overborne by the temptations of alcohol, predisposed to them by fatigue. Or he may be alive and strong in body, mind and morals, but condemned by the nature of his employment to long and recurring idleness without income. Irregularity of work and earnings is a characteristic experience of modern industrial life. In these cases the normal arrangement is inverted, and industry invades the home in search of the labor of the crippled, the bedridden, and the mothers of little children. Thus because industry has developed, bringing in its train underpay, irregularity, disease and death, and because our industrial code does not yet protect the family, widows and young children are forced to take upon themselves the burden of manufacture in the home under the sweating system.

The cruel old decision of the Court of Appeals of New York still stands unchanged since the Jacobs case. The manufacturer's right to invade with his materials the homes of the tenement dwellers can be restricted only when the interest of the health of the public in the restriction is obvious to the Court. It was, therefore, deemed wiser in 1913, not to include in a list of industries to be banished by statute from the tenements garments intended for adults! Children are admittedly endangered by germs transmitted in tenement homework. Any gain to the family life of the workers, any freeing of their homes from invasion by industry, must be clearly subordinate to safeguarding the health of purchasers, lest the Court hold the new law contrary to the constitution.

Ownership of the Home

Incredible sacrifices have been made by millions of families for the sake of home ownership.

As long ago as the days of Martin Chuzzlewit, Charles Dickens revealed a painful aspect of the real estate gambling which has preyed upon this effort.

More recently, great manufacturing corporations in villages and small cities have developed from this an effective trap, encouraging employés to buy homes, and so chaining them to the spot. The owners of homes partly paid for dare not strike, lest they lose all the payments they have made. In Auburn, in 1913, the Harvester Works threatened its striking employés that the works might be permanently removed. That would mean the loss of the employés' whole investment in Auburn, a city of homes.

An opposite method of attaining the same end is the generation long policy of coal-carrying roads and coal companies, in Pennsylvania and West Virginia, where the workers are perforce tenants of their employers. In Westmoreland, Pennsylvania, the evicted striking miners lived for months in tents lent them by other working men in the hard winter and late spring of 1912. In the winter and spring of 1913 a similar experience has befallen the miners in West Virginia. Whole communities, evicted by coal companies, have camped in tents lent them by the mineworkers' union. Evicted wives and newborn babies of skilled miners died of cold and exposure in the midst of the coal fields—a grewsome irony of modern industry.

By their onslaughts on the family life of miners the coal mining companies and the coal carrying roads may contribute to end the private ownership of coal mines, to make coal a national possession, and coal mining and coal carrying a national service.

Having thus briefly and fragmentarily indicated the disintegrating effect of modern industry upon the family as exemplified in the experience of fathers, mothers, children, young daughters working at night, and the home itself (in the sense of physical shelter), there remains—underlying all family life—the means of subsistence.

The Wage Scale

In a steadily growing proportion of the American nation, the economic foundation of the family is the wage scale. While our ideal of the home remains agricultural we have become, also, an industrial people largely dependent upon wages. And the wage scale in private industry we have left to be determined by the play of competition.

A single fact brought to light last year illumines ironically the relation of modern industry to the wage earning family. Dr. Caroline Hedger, of the

Chicago University Settlement, discovered that
children in the neighborhood of the Chicago
stockyards are fed coffee because their parents
cannot afford milk for them. Fathers and mothers who spend their lives in killing cattle and
packing meat, to feed this nation and Europe,
cannot afford for their own children milk in in-
fancy. In the midst of more cows than are
brought together anywhere else, babies are fed
coffee for its cheapness. The railroads' profit on
hauling milk to the city, the milk trust's dividend
derived from distributing milk in the stockyards
district, the milk retailers' profit upon their share
of this work, and the meagre wage paid to men
and women who prepare a staple food for adults,
together result in robbing these babies altogether
of their most necessary food.

Competitive determination of wage scales is
less endurable from decade to decade. Therefore
we see our fellow citizens swarming into the federal civil service in quest of permanent salaries,
and into state and city employments lured by the
twofold attraction of permanent employment and
retiring pensions, however modest both may be.
Or they seek arbitration of their wage disputes
under the Erdman Act, or demand the creation
of minimum wage boards, at least for women and
minors.

Why do we Americans not frankly copy the good democratic method worked out by the Australians since 1896, and adopted with some modifications in England since 1910? They creàte in an underpaid industry a board composed of representatives, elected by employers and by employés, who meet and consider payrolls and the cost of living. In the full light of publicity these representatives of the parties in interest arrive at an agreement which, if approved by the appropriate supervising authority, is thereafter binding upon both for an agreed time. At the end of the time, either side may ask for a change and the negotiations may begin anew.

Our American spirit in relation to such legislation is undemocratic. Although minimum wage laws are intended to confirm the economic foundation of the family and check the process of disintegration, the members of families most concerned are not necessarily to be consulted according to our present initial statutes.

Men are omitted from these new laws upon an arbitrary assumption that the laws would be unconstitutional if applied to men. Why do we Americans refuse to face the fact that women and minors are earning wages primarily because of underpaid husbands and fathers, who would gladly keep their wives at home and their children in school? That it is precisely in the interest of the family that the wages of men should be regulated?

Our new statutes do not, as in Australia, usually provide for election of members of the boards, a safeguard of the interests of wageworkers, which experience has shown to be useful. Unhappily, this new institution of wage boards thus tends, in one state after another, to become an eleemosynary arrangement confined to women and minors, instead of a democratic method of constraining industry to pay its just debts from week to week, to afford an honest and sufficient family livelihood to all people, men and women alike, who do honest work. Why do we not, at the beginning of public regulation of wages, strengthen the economic foundations of family life by providing that men and women may be elected to represent their fellow workers, meeting upon wage boards the representatives of employers (elected by the employers), the whole group bringing to bear the collective wisdom of all upon the difficult subject of the payroll?

Regenerative Forces Within the Family

Within the family itself, two regenerative forces are slowly becoming manifest, the consumers' growing consciousness of power over industry, and the increasing numbers of enfranchised women.

English, German, Belgian and Swiss families have set an example to the rest of the world by building up cooperative enterprises, retail distributive at first, and now spreading powerfully in the fields of wholesale distribution and manufacture. Through these agencies cooperating families lower prices, raise qualities, and standardize conditions of employment in relation to the articles consumed in their homes. Incidentally they compel their non-cooperative competitors to approach more or less closely the same improved standards.

England has in its federated cooperative societies nearly three million members, men and women, whose capital amounts to more than two and a half billion dollars wholly invested in cooperative enterprises. Through this movement, a large proportion of the domestic consumption of the families is covered.

The German societies report a membership of more than five and a half million, and an annual turnover of a billion and a quarter dollars.

The admirable social achievement of the Belgian cooperatives is too well known to require more than a passing reference.

The Ninth International Cooperative Congress,

held at Glasgow in 1913, reports delegates from
24 nations, in which there are more than twenty
million members of cooperative societies. Of
these six millions are within the bodies organically
affiliated with the International Cooperative Al-
liance.

The improved quality of the cooperators themselves is increasingly recognized as of greater importance than their industrial achievement.
Their self-confidence, business ability, and active
participation in the control of industry have no
parallel among us. In using this vast power at
their command as consumers, American families
have strangely lagged behind. Here is a promis-
ing field of activity ignored by those wives of pro-
fessional men, and better paid employés, whose
economic activities have gone from the home, and
whose enforced leisure is not altogether a source
of satisfaction.

Though the vast majority of consumers are
themselves workers—farmers or wage earners—
they have not yet generally perceived that the
tendency of the family to disintegrate has for its
final cause the lost ownership of their tools by the
workers. The civilized world is, however, gradually coming to see that it can never return to the
primitive ownership of the agricultural period.
The perception spreads from nation to nation that

the growing control of industry by those who work —brain workers and hand workers—means henceforth not direct, individual possession, but an immeasurable variety of forms of participation in cooperative ownership, public and private.

In America voting women are increasing from year to year and revealing the regenerative power of the ballot in the service of the family. Four and a half million women vote in Washington, Oregon, California, Arizona, Utah, Idaho, Alaska, Wyoming, Colorado, Kansas, and Illinois; and in thirteen other states the process of enfranchising women will reach the stage of referendum to the voters before the election of the next President in 1916. Already wage earning women and girls in Arizona, Washington, California, Colorado and the District of Columbia enjoy the benefits of the eight hours day; and in Washington, Oregon, Utah, Colorado, and California minimum wage laws for them have, with their help as voters, been enacted, an epoch making innovation, even though these laws are still experimental and in need of improvement. It seems reasonable to believe that these are mere intimations of the measures of self-defence of the family which are destined to be established by means of new powers gradually being conferred upon women.

An infinite vista opens before the mind, of regenerative power for the restoration and progress of the family through the development of cooperation and community action in the industrial field. The era of unbridled power exercised by irresponsible industry at cost of the family—the fundamental institution of the human race—is slowly drawing to a close.

Hence the vital strength of the rapidly growing movement to extend all devices of democratic government. When the coming worldwide industrial code for restoring and safeguarding the family is at length adopted in its fullness, it will express the will of the adult people whom it concerns, men and women together. In that direction lies hope of regeneration of the family under the conditions created by modern industry.

II

MODERN INDUSTRY IN RELATION TO HEALTH

MODERN INDUSTRY AND HEALTH

Modern industry offers, in abundance new to human experience, everything requisite for the enjoyment of good health. It produces unmeasured wealth in myriad forms—food, clothing, shelter, books, the means of travel, recreation and enjoyment.

For fighting disease, too, the arsenal was never so well furnished. Every year we have more hospitals, more costly and more splendid, more sanatoria, more clinics, more medical schools, more training schools for nurses. Endowments for research increase and the discoveries from their laboratories follow each other in hope-inspiring succession. Crusades against disease are carried forward, nationwide in scope, against tuberculosis, infant mortality, cancer, blindness, the social diseases, and insanity.

From year to year the social functions of doctors and nurses are extended. School doctors and school nurses are already an old story, their beneficent work is recognized as indispensable, and

41

their ranks are now increased by their colleagues
attached to municipal milk stations. Nursing the
poor in their homes has been, for more than a decade, a municipal activity in Los Angeles, and has
recently celebrated its twentieth anniversary as a
voluntary activity in New York City. We are
growing accustomed to the presence of nurses in
department stores and factories, to follow-up
nurses from the hospitals, and to nursing in connection with industrial insurance.

It is the new wealth created by modern industry which makes possible this nationwide war
upon disease.

This is, moreover, only a part of the cheerful
tale. Industry affords, almost from day to day,
fresh resources for making work healthful and
pleasant. Improvements in the production of
concrete, steel and glass, and advances in engineer-
ing, make possible the construction of factories
fireproof and perfectly lighted, ventilated, and
heated. Where the outside air is vitiated, it can
be purified by artificial means while it is brought
indoors, and this is increasingly done for commercial purposes. Electrical vacuum processes draw
off dust at the point at which it is generated, so
that neither the particular workman engaged at
a machine hitherto a dangerous dust generator,
nor his colleague working in the same room, need

henceforth suffer from dust. By the use of suitable glass shades, electric light can now be tempered to the human eye. Seats of all kinds and heights are ready on the market. The list of resources made available by industry itself for making work wholesome and agreeable can be prolonged indefinitely.

Normally industry itself should be an upbuilding process, a daily benefit to mind and body of all who participate in it. Every sound man and woman is physically the better for regular active work. Rational exertion with moderate leisure, and assured livelihood without worry about daily bread, naturally conduce to good health. And for all these things modern industry amply provides the raw materials. Never before were the technical conditions so favorable for assuring to all who work reasonably short hours (to avoid the stupefying effects of monotony and speeding) cheering rewards, and the consciousness of useful service.

With the help of modern hygiene and preventive medicine, enriched by all the new resources, we ought to be living in vigor and enjoyment on our seventieth birthdays, unless we are cut down by the enemy in the form of inoperable cancer, or some obscure disease of the heart, or by one of the mysterious maladies whose secrets science has not yet laid bare. Indeed, Professor Metschnikoff has long encouraged us to hope that our great-grandchildren may live in physical vigor far beyond the century mark. And certain life insurance companies are collecting data about centenarian policy holders.

At present, however, the average age at death of the American people, in the registration area, is approximately 47 years instead of the Biblical three score years and ten, or the 140 years held out to the hopes of our successors by the head of the Pasteur Institute.

Disease and Death By-products of Industry

It is the paradox of modern industry in relation to health that, while producing the wealth which enriches medical institutions and sustains the professions of scientific research, medicine and nursing, it gives rise to a considerable part of the disease which they strive to cure, and the deaths which they aim to defer. Avoidable disease and premature death are among its regular by-products, and it exhausts ever widening ranges of working people. It exerts a continuous injurious influence upon masses of those who consume its products, or work in its service.

These sinister facts have been slow to attract widespread attention because we lack the two

essential sources of knowledge about them—vital
statistics and insurance records.

We are the one great nation without vital statistics. We do not know how many children are
born each year in our Republic, or how many
people die.

The first service of the federal Children's Bureau
in the initial year of its activity consists in forc-
ing upon the attention of the nation the fact that,
of our forty-eight states, only eight register births
in accordance with the standard set by the Federal
Census Bureau.* These are the New England
states with Pennsylvania and Michigan. In New
York the vital statistics are good enough to bring
the city within the registration area. But it is
easier to get birth certificates for little Turks born
in Turkey, than for American children born in
the rural counties of New York State when the
children apply for "working papers," and their
birth certificates are their first requisite.

After the vital statistics which we lack, the second available source of exact knowledge of the

* These states were admitted to the "provisional registration
area." Not all of them have complete registration. New
laws go into effect (1914) in Arkansas, North Carolina, and
Tennessee, and amendments in some other states. It is not
possible to say whether their results will be satisfactory until
they have had sufficient time to give a fair test, there are so
many conditions affecting the completeness of returns.

relation of disease to industry would be the records of social insurance such as Germany has been accumulating throughout a quarter century. In the coal mining areas and textile manufacturing districts in Germany, the births and deaths of children, and the age at death, and causes of death, of their fathers are known through vital statistics and social insurance records. The relative dangers to life and health in these two great industries can, therefore, be accurately traced.

For the corresponding coal mining areas of West Virginia and textile manufacturing districts of New Jersey, we know nothing trustworthy as to birth, death, health or disease of children or parents. So, too, in regard to the stockyards region of Chicago, the second city of the nation. Although it is a matter of common knowledge that children born in that part of the city die in great numbers very young, we have no scientific, official statement.

After a nationwide crusade lasting ten years, we have no adequate registration of a disease so omnipresent as tuberculosis.

We have no national policy with regard to health, and no scientific basis for the adoption of such a policy. The absence of vital statistics indicates correctly our national indifference to the whole subject. Indeed, in recent years an effort

to create a federal Department of Health with a
representative in the Cabinet has called forth horrifying opposition.

Under these circumstances of national indifference to life and health, our belated state in regard
to social insurance follows naturally. The first
American conference on the subject occurred in
1913, and the tenth biennial meeting of the International Conference, which will be held in the
United States in 1915, will be the first session held
in this country. Social insurance records are,
thus, for us wholly a hope for the future.

All these difficulties being duly recognized, it is
still true that, at least within the registration area,
we know enough in regard to deaths to venture
certain conclusions. Among these the most important is that, within that area, the death rate
is too slowly declining, the average life is too
slowly lengthening.

After living more than twenty years in working
class districts of two leading industrial cities, New
York and Chicago, I am impressed with the deadly
effects, in working class families, of two active
continuing influences—the bad food supply, and
the ignorant mothers in relation to that supply.
Whatever progress has been achieved in prolong-
ing human life by reducing mortality of infants

and young children is due to efforts directly counteracting these agencies.

Commercialized Food

In certain cities charitable societies and boards of health afford, through a limited number of milk stations, supplies especially provided for the children of the poor and warranted not to kill or injure them. But for the general supply consumed by families who are neither rich enough to buy certified milk, nor poor enough for charity, we set a standard too low for health, too high for the farmers under present railway charges. Why have we not good milk for all, since the technical knowledge necessary for obtaining it is now everywhere available?

A chief difficulty is an industrial one, the slow service and excessive charges of railroads. These discourage farmers from enlarging their output, and in great measure spoil the product in transit, by exposing it to prolonged heat in summer, and by tempting shippers to drug milk with preservatives.

Retail dealers constitute a second great difficulty in the way of a wholesome urban milk supply for all the children. They keep up the price, and succumb to temptation to spoil milk as food for babies by adding water or preservatives (for-

maldehyde and others) to their own profit. They
add germs of malignant disease when milk is sold
in little shops that are the front rooms of dwellings in which there happens to be illness. And
their dirty ways often add to milk filth bacteria
that are fatal, particularly during hot weather,
to little children and to invalids. Such hordes of
milk retailers are licensed, that no one can pos-
sibly know how they conduct their business day by
day and hour by hour. Yet this is a matter of
life and death for children.

Before infant mortality can be reduced to its
possible minimum, the milk industry must, in the
interest of all children in all city homes, be municipal like the water supply, and like it safe and
abundant. Although this change obviously cannot be complete until American railroads are, like
the Swiss railroads, public servants of the people,
hopeful beginnings exist in the municipal milk
stations of New York, Rochester, and a few other
cities.

Minor industrial causes of infant mortality are
worthless baby foods, poisonous soothing syrups,
and long rubbered feeding bottles. For children
a few years older, at the kindergarten and primary
school age, industry purveys candy, soda water
and ice-cream in which glue, lampblack, glucose,
sulphurous acid, saccharin, paraffin, coal-tar dyes,

and many poisonous coloring matters are ingredients. It is chiefly boys and girls of wage earning families who buy them, often as substitutes for regular meals, spending for them pennies left for food by a mother whose occupation keeps her away from home at meal times. Children who buy these substitutes for food do so habitually. Their appetite for wholesome food is cloyed, their digestion clogged, and malnutrition follows.

It is hard to conceive of a city or state producing and distributing substances like these. And the question, therefore, arises in behalf of the most dependent, defenceless members of the community, how long our food supply is to be entrusted to adulterators and speculators?

There is a widespread misapprehension as to the degree of protection afforded to the public by the federal pure food law. All the substances above enumerated are debarred from interstate commerce if shipped for use as food. But they can be legally manufactured and sold locally, unless state laws or city ordinances against them are enacted and enforced.

All these injurious articles are sold to New York City school children in the immediate vicinity of school buildings. They are manufactured and consumed within the city, and therefore escape the national pure food and drug law.

The same exemption applies to tuberculous milk and meat if produced and sold locally. Every state is free to legislate or not as it sees fit, and every community is a law unto itself in the matter of enforcement. In the whole country, only three cities have municipal slaughter houses. In these the city naturally determines the method of preparing the meat supply, and the state laws can obviously be enforced without incentive to resistance or evasion. If the municipal abattoirs were supplemented with city markets suitably placed, one important element of the food problem of wage-earning families in those cities would be greatly simplified.

Ignorant Mothers

Physicians and nurses working in connection with milk stations agree that their most useful service consists in educating mothers in the care of babies and young children. For of what avail is it to get certified milk into the tenements, an expensive and laborious process, if the mothers then leave it exposed to heat, bad air and flies? Or if they continue, as before, to feed the babies coffee, cucumbers and pickles?

The cause of the mothers' ignorance is usually the insufficient wage of the family breadwinner which in industrial communities urges the young girls to leave school from grades below that in which domestic science instruction even begins. In the great Southern cotton manufacturing states—in Georgia, Alabama, the Carolinas— where children enter the mills exceptionally at seven and eight years, and in great numbers at eleven and twelve, their minds are not mature enough to profit by such instruction as future mothers need for the safety and welfare of their children.

From the point of view, however, of the life and health of the next generation, the employment of little girls in mills is hardly more injurious than the exhausting and stupefying work of older ones, from fourteen to twenty. An industrial Republic needs highly intelligent mothers, capable of taking care of the health of all the members of the family, of whom the babies are merely the most sensitive and perishable. For this reason the public welfare requires that all working girls should be kept in attendance at part time continuation schools far beyond the present limit of sixteen years of age, whatever modification of workroom schedules and of existing curricula this may involve.

The disease most common among working people, tuberculosis, is cultivated by wholesale in the tenement home and in the workroom. Crowded sleeping rooms, broken rest, insufficient, ill prepared, unsuitable food at home cooperate with fatigue, dust, strain in the workroom to prepare the bodies of workers, particularly of the young, to receive the germ under circumstances favorable to its development. Nightwork especially predisposes the young frame to welcome the plague, for sleep lost at night cannot be made up in a working class district.

Tuberculosis is a mass product of modern industry. Yet in our crusade against it we have, hitherto, used retail measures. The crusade has, therefore, no such sweeping reduction in cases to report as its founders hoped and foretold a decade ago. The industrial predisposing causes are all still in force—poverty, fatigue, tuberculous meat and milk on the market, bad housing, and congestion of population.*

Wages and Health

The cost of living has increased in recent years, and the standard of living has fallen, certainly for the unskilled, the common laborers.

* It will be a matter of literally vital interest to watch the activities of the newly enfranchised women in San Francisco, Los Angeles and Chicago as to the public health in these aspects—the care of the food supply, the education of girls for family life, and the solution of the hitherto insoluble housing problem.

In the minds of working people the world over there has never been a doubt that, for their health, the most important consideration is the standard of living, steady income, rational in relation to the cost of food, clothing, shelter. Hence their innumerable strikes for increased wages.

Unhappily, the workers have not hitherto controlled this relation, for how do they profit by an increased wage in the cases in which they succeed in getting it, if the increase all goes to the landlord, the meat trust, the coal trust, the milkman? Without scientific distribution of the necessaries of life as pure and cheap as our existing technic makes possible, the increase becomes illusory. This long-delayed expansion of public functions we are justified in expecting of the new voters of whom so large a proportion are self-supporting, or the wives of wage-earning men.

As important for the public health as for the restoration of the family is the new interference of the public in the determination of wages. It has become a matter of almost annual recurrence that the federal government intervenes between some large congeries of railroads and their organized employés to maintain the standard of wages. The new state commissions on women's wages are obviously destined to contribute towards preventing tuberculosis and insanity by assuring a livelihood, however modest, to women workers who have proverbially worked the longest hours, at the most wearing tasks, for the most wretched pay.

The present conflagration of interest and alarm concerning the wages of women and girls in relation to the public health and morals was kindled in greater degree than is commonly known by the modest little volume, Making Both Ends Meet, by Edith Wyatt and Sue Ainslie Clark,* which embodied facts gathered directly from some hundreds of women and girls living away from their families and supporting themselves. Its publication stimulated some of the earliest direct efforts in this country for wage legislation.

Preventable Dangers in Industry

The characteristic of modern industry is incessant change. As old processes are abandoned and new ones introduced, new dangers, new injurious influences constantly arise, and new powers of controlling them as well. Among the incidents of industry varying from branch to branch, from place to place, are heat, cold, glare, darkness, in-

* Macmillan, 1910. Miss Wyatt is Vice-President of the Consumers' League of Illinois, and Miss Ainslie made her investigation while one of the secretaries of the National Consumers' League.

sufficient lighting, noise, speeding, monotony, heavy lifting, standing, bad air, dampness, contact with poisonous materials, dangerous machinery, and processes generating dust, gases and vapors.

These industrial menaces to the health of wage-earners are discussed in ever fresh editions of foreign standard works on industrial hygiene. It is a striking and discreditable fact that we have, in the United States, no standard work on this infinitely important subject. We are dependent upon the English writers, Sir Thomas Oliver and Hutchins and Harrison, although, in many important respects, conditions are so different in the two countries that these valuable works are in part inapplicable here.*

Indeed, it is only because of the default of science in this field that a lay observer finds a re-

* The first American monographs dealing with special aspects of industrial disease are still recent, Dr. Alice Hamilton's studies of lead poisoning, published by the U. S. Department of Labor, and Dr. John B. Andrews' investigation of the use of white sulphur in manufacturing matches.

Two valuable state reports dealing with more general aspects of health and industry are those of the Mass. State Board of Health (1907) and the more recent Illinois State Commission on the Health, Safety and Comfort of Employés.

The New York State Factories Investigating Commission, also, in its current reports contributes valuable data.

spectful hearing. It is as a lay observer that I
venture to report the following observations incidental to my work as factory inspector for the
State of Illinois, or as visitor for the National
Consumers' League, or as one (for a brief month)
of the members of the staff of the Pittsburgh
Survey.

In Chicago, at the Stockyards, in 1895, on an
August day so hot that three employés died of
sunstroke, young immigrant boys were serving as
door-openers of the cooling rooms. A boy opening a door for little electric trains carrying sides
of beef, was—as the door swung open—exposed
to the scorching heat of the outside world. Then
—as the train slowly passed him—the door swing-
ing inward—he returned to his post inside the
cooling room where icicles hung from the ceiling
because that temperature was necessary for the
meat. All day long, he oscillated between those
extremes of temperature. Cynical, indeed, was
the contrast between the provision for the well-
being of the beef, and the exposure of the immigrant boys to pneumonia or rheumatism!

If there is, to-day, any regulation of temperature at the Chicago Stockyards in the interest of
the health of employés, it has been achieved
through enforcement of the Health, Safety and

Comfort Act, under the new administration, and within the past few months.

In Pittsburgh, the Black City, a department store exhibits marvellous laces, and delicately tinted, perishable silks. The soot laden city air is drawn down through a high intake, and kept physically pure by being pumped through flowing water and cotton batting. In this store are to be found the most uniformly courteous, unwearied, refreshed looking sales clerks in all the city. When I commented upon this fact to the manager, he agreed that pure, fresh air undoubtedly was one contributing cause of this desirable condition. "But," he said, "it is only honest to tell you that we did that in the first place for the sake of the laces and silks."

In a candy factory in the same Black City of Pittsburgh, I found on a horribly smoky, muggy September afternoon, in 1907, a workroom so cool and refreshing, in which everyone looked so comfortable, that I have always remembered it as a bright spot in a dismal experience. The workroom was kept at a fixed temperature and the air pure because the girls were dipping chocolates of the finest and most expensive quality which would be ruined if the heat and soot of the city reached them. For that one room the air was pumped through cotton batting and cold, flowing water and, by a fortunate accident, the temperature required for the chocolates happened also to be wholesome and agreeable for the workers. The closing gong sounded while we lingered in the room, and the girls showed no zeal to rush for their hats and quit the place. I spoke of this to one of them, and her quick reply was "Do you think we're going to be as comfortable as this again before we get back here to-morrow morning?"

Surely the time cannot be far distant when the conscience of the community will demand of the chocolate industry that it shall do throughout, for the health and comfort of its workers, what it now finds it profitable to do in one room in each factory for the sake of the appearance of its product.

In a southern city, in the heart of a vast tobacco growing region, I was taken to see a new candy factory of which the citizens were proud. It was in a fine new concrete building, with innumerable windows admitting light and air. These were open in the mild southern climate, and a swarm of bees had entered through them in search of sweets. A battle was going on between the employés and the bees, and the floor was strewn with dead and wounded insects. To me as representative of the consuming public, this floor was of extraordinary interest. It was of light-colored concrete, smooth and adapted to the maintenance of exquisite cleanliness. The manager had provided numerous spittoons for the use of the workmen. Neither he nor they seemed, however, to feel under obligation to use them, and the light-colored, smooth concrete floor was disfigured in many directions with pools of tobacco juice, through which flies and surviving wounded bees crawled in great numbers, crawling afterwards over candy in various stages of preparation and packing.

In this new factory the latest machinery was installed. Here, too, the chocolate room was kept at a fixed temperature. The candies were of all qualities, from fine bon-bons to the poisonous trash which mission Sunday schools buy for their Christmas trees. Coal-tar dyes of many colors stood boldly open to view, and our friendly host offered us candies to eat, unconscious of the horror inspired by his defiled floor, his spittoons, and his coal-tar dyes.

There was, at that time, no state factory law, and no requirement that seats should be provided for women and girls at work. A large group of young girls, apparently between 14 and 16 years of age stood, packing candy for shipment, at a table far too high for them, which had been originally adapted to a group of men who were now working in a different part of the factory. To our suggestion that the girls could do more work in a day if the table were lowered and they were allowed to sit, the manager genially replied that they were paid by the piece and worked as hard as they could, whatever position they were in. The concrete floor, which so sadly failed of its purpose in the matter of cleanliness, was terribly hard upon the feet of all who had to stand long upon it. Needless standing is always an indication of incompetent management. It is less injurious to boys than to girls because of their different structure, and because they are so inevitably restless that they shift about and lessen the harm to themselves without knowing that they are doing it. Their very restlessness often saves them from being asked to stand except when actively engaged in tending a machine which automatically keeps them still.

That factory ships candy in quantities throughout the Southwest, and the people of the city in which it stands buy its product with pride and pleasure because it is the most modern of their industries. The manager is a much respected, enterprising citizen, no more aware of the relation of industry to health and disease than the people among whom he moves socially.

How far we are from acting upon the idea that work is one foundation of health, how much farther from compelling industry to use its own inherent resources for the good health of the workers, is illustrated by an episode of the Pittsburgh Survey. During an early conference of the investigators, in September, 1907, someone suggested that one of the first inquiries should test the truth of the statement that, in the steel industry, men were employed 365 days in the year, twelve hours a day; and twice a month 24 hours at a stretch, at the turn of the shift from nightwork to daywork on Sunday. All who were present agreed, except the questioner, that it seemed inconceivable that men could endure such strain, especially in the heat at which much of the work is done.

After a fortnight, however, Professor Commons reported that it was true. Those were the working hours, for the water boys as well as for the men whom they served, and the consequences were such as would naturally follow. Occasionally a man died at his work. Sometimes a man collapsed on the way home. Strained hearts, paralysis, and disorders less obviously traceable to a particular exertion but due to heat, fatigue, and strain carried men off.

The steel industry did not, at that time, get

many local recruits among Americans, or among
foreigners who had been here any length of time.
Employment bureaus were maintained to bring in
men from Ellis Island to Pittsburgh, to work
under that strain.

When the facts were ascertained and made public, conditions began very slowly to change in
some degree. Sunday repair work was reduced
in some places; shifts were, in some cases, changed
from two of twelve hours to three of eight hours
each, though 63 per cent. of employés in the steel
industry still worked 12 hours in 24 in the year
1913.

The stockholders of the industry have again
voted against a general reduction of the working
hours to eight; and the legislature of Pennsylvania has again killed a bill which would, if
enacted, have ended the employment at night of
boys fourteen and fifteen years old in making
steel.

Neither the federal government, the State of
Pennsylvania, nor the City of Pittsburgh has
records showing what this overwork has been doing to the health of the workers. When men fell
ill of tuberculosis, rheumatism, or other slow dis-
abling disease, they commonly went home to
Europe to die, so that they did not even appear

in the mortality figures of the decennial federal Census.

The steel industry had been encouraged in recklessness by a decision of the Supreme Court of Pennsylvania. If an alien was killed in industry, the surviving alien dependents living in Europe could not through counsel, or through the consul of their own country, appear in any court in Pennsylvania to ask damages for the loss of their breadwinner. This has recently been altered by statute, so that to-day, if a Slav or an Italian comes to this country leaving his family in Europe and is killed while still an alien, his family may claim damages.

Sinister, indeed, for a series of years, was the influence of that decision upon the health and safety of workingmen in Pennsylvania. To avoid the possible costs entailed by the death of native or naturalized men while at work, employment agents bringing in recruits for the dangerous industries were actively tempted by the decision to prefer detached aliens.

Our greatest manufacturing industry was, under that decision, moving in the direction exactly opposite to that of Germany and the other most enlightened industrial nations. They have, for a quarter century, been striving to stimulate employers to make industry safe by increasingly placing upon them the cost of the death or dis-

ability of a wage earner. The employers, under
this compulsion, form mutual insurance companies and distribute over the whole industry, as they
see fit, the damage cost arising from deaths and
injuries. Such insurance affords the maximum
financial stimulus for employers to make industry
safe. The Pennsylvania decision worked for
years in exactly the opposite way.

Among several states which are now legislating
with intent to make industry safe, perhaps the
most striking experiment is that of Washington.
The statute provides that if, in any occupation,
an employé loses his life or becomes permanently
disabled, his dependents have a valid, legal claim
upon that industry—the wife throughout widowhood, the children until the 16th birthday.

This statute has been unanimously sustained by
the Supreme Court of Washington, and is pending
before the Supreme Court of the United States, in
a case to test its constitutionality. There was in
the state one extra hazardous industry, the manufacture of explosives. Only two establishments
were engaged in it. One blew up, killing eight
employés. The State of Washington paid the
damages due, under the statute, to the survivors
and to the dependents of the dead, and sent the
bill to the company and its competitor. The competitor is testing the constitutionality of the law.

No other state seems to have gone quite so far as Washington in its effort to make it worth while for the extra hazardous industries to reduce their hazards. The decision of the Supreme Court of the United States will, therefore, be of epoch making importance.

Between the extremes of policy adopted by Washington on the one hand, and the courts of Pennsylvania on the other (whose decisions have, for years, deprived thousands of working people of compensation for injuries) experiments in great variety are in process, all directed toward assuring to wage workers and their families some compensation, and to employers new stimulus for making industry safe.

Any constitution can, with the expenditure of time and trouble, be brought into line with civilization.* Laws must ultimately be enacted in every state, assuring to the survivors of men killed at work some payment of damages, and to workers hurt but not killed some reasonable compensation for the loss of health, or limbs, or earning power. In not one state has this yet been done effectively.

If the Supreme Court of the United States fol-

* This has been conclusively shown by the action of the voters of New York State during the past three years in relation to workmen's compensation.

lows the reasoning of the Court of Washington, the slow process of changing constitutions and statutes of other states will be relatively easy. If, however, the Supreme Court of the United States should follow the reasoning of the New York Court of Appeals in the Ives case, we shall be confronted by the painful and weary task of amending the Constitution of the United States. The recent adoption of two amendments, the first in nearly fifty years, shows that this process, though slow and discouraging, is no longer impossible.

Factory Inspection

One serious weakness in our dealing with industry in relation to health, safety and comfort lies in our disregard of the factory inspection staff. In Germany, where accidents and bad health among employés are causes of direct expense to employers, the aid and advice of inspectors are sought for keeping factories safe and wholesome. Inspectors are technically trained men and women, carefully fitted for their work and of great importance to both employers and employés. Their visits are, therefore, welcomed by both.

In this country, on the contrary, inspectors are selected in consideration of their usefulness to a party organization, or a trade union, rather than their technical qualifications for their task. In

the greatest industrial state, New York, where the
inspection staff has the nominal protection of the
civil service law, the State Civil Service Commission has, for many years, been as actively in poli-
tics as any avowedly political part of the state
government. This is utterly demoralizing to the
inspection staff and the employers, and defeats the
purpose for which the inspectors exist.

Twenty years ago, I cherished hopes of improved provisions for the health of factory workers to come through the employment of women
as inspectors. Experience has shown that there
is a large field in which they can be of great service. But neither men nor women can do what
needs to be done until our whole attitude toward
the task is fundamentally changed. At present,
the employés are so hopeless of benefits to be derived from the visits of inspectors, that they are
commonly either wholly indifferent or, sometimes,
willing cynically to join with foreman or superintendent in tricking an inspector and concealing
violations of the law.

A black chapter in our industrial history is this
of our treatment of our factory inspectors. They
have been left in the position of hostile critics—
prosecutors—of corporations infinitely more powerful than themselves. Within the factory they
have been met as enemies, bribed when possible

and, in shamefully numerous cases, removed from office when they could be neither bribed, tricked nor intimidated.

Under these sorry conditions the scientific output of these officials is naturally valueless. Indeed, with the honorable exception of the New York State reports standardized a few years ago by Commissioner Sherman, the official reports on factory inspection only deepen the darkness of our ignorance of the relation of the different branches of industry to the health of the workers or the consumers.

Fatigue and Disease

During the past three-quarters of a century there has been a continuous movement for a shorter working day. When, in 1830, my father was a printer's apprentice in Philadelphia, he and his fellow apprentices regularly expected to work in summer "from light until dark," i. e. from the moment they could see after dawn, until they could no longer see in the late dusk of the summer evening. In winter they worked from 6 a. m. to 8 p. m. with an hour for dinner, and a half hour each for breakfast and supper.

During the three-quarters of a century since those days, hundreds of thousands of men and women have engaged in strikes in the hope of establishing permanently a shorter working day. In so doing, they were performing, at a terrible cost to themselves, an invaluable service in behalf of the public health of this nation. But this fact was not recognized until within recent years, and then only incidentally. Even now it appears probable that far more would have been gained, and at infinitely less cost in suffering, if the energy spent in strikes for shorter working hours had all been directed to enacting and enforcing statutes.

Since 1895, the Supreme Court of the United States has, at different times and in connection with several cases, laid down the principle that the welfare of the community requires some reasonable restriction upon the working hours of adult men and women. The Court decided in 1898,* that the working day might reasonably be limited to eight hours for men working underground in mines and smelters. This could be done because mining was an intrinsically dangerous occupation. Later, the Court held † that the working hours of bakers could not be limited by statute to ten in twenty-four. For if baking had been an intrinsically dangerous occupation, the women who have, since the foundation of the Republic, baked bread for their families, must have suffered

* Holden vs. Hardy, 169 U. S. 366.
† Lochner vs. New York, 198 U. S. 45, 1905.

in health. The Court was not acquainted with the trade life of bakers. It did not know that, in American cities, thousands of bakers work underground, almost like miners.

In this decision the Court laid down the principle that, where a statute interferes with the freedom of contract of adults, professedly in the interest of the public health and welfare, the fact must be made clear to the Court that the public health is really concerned.

In this decision began the recent era of sustained, continuing effort for a working day limited by statute for men and women in manufacture. Upon this decision rests the procedure of the National Consumers' League whose Committee on the Legal Defence of Labor Laws has since 1907 continuously prepared briefs for the use of the courts in cases involving working hours.*

In the preparation of these briefs the fact has been discovered and popularized that, of all the industrial causes of disease, none is so universal

* Fatigue and Efficiency, by Josephine Goldmark. The Russell Sage Foundation, 1912. This fundamental work dealing with the relation of fatigue to disease grew out of a brief prepared by Miss Goldmark in defence of the Oregon ten hours' law for women employed in manufacture. The brief formed the basis of the favorable decision handed down in January, 1908, by the Supreme Court of the United States.

as fatigue.   Of all the poisons, it is the most universally diffused, controllable but not to-day controlled.   Sinister as many industrial poisons are now known to be, this one alone invests with a deadly threat the common run of ordinary occupations.   This gives new significance to the complaint that working people are worn out prematurely by simple tasks, if these tasks involve monotony or speeding.

We know now for the first time, in a form clear not only to learned courts, but to the simplest machine tenders, *why* these are often old at thirty, and superannuated at forty years.   The omnipresent poison of fatigue prepares the frames for every germ that lurks.

This consideration it is which led the Supreme Court of Mississippi to speak recently of the "inalienable right to rest," in a decision sustaining as constitutional a statute limiting to ten hours the working day of men and women in cotton mills.

The whole procedure in defence of labor laws has thus been revolutionized.   Instead of abstract discussions of abstract freedom, the procedure is, to-day, to ascertain the exact facts, to show what the existing working hours are, what other nations and states have done about it, and what the medical profession says on the subject.   The final deciding factor is not "freedom" but health.

The International Conference for Labor Legislation at Berne, Switzerland, in September, 1913, had for its principal subjects two proposals dealing with working hours. One was the introduction of the ten hours days for women in manufacture in all the fourteen nations of Europe, by a treaty like that which took effect on New Year's Day, 1910, and assured to all women so employed a period of 11 hours' rest at night, of which seven hours must fall between 10 p. m. and 5 a. m.

The second proposal was to extend to boys below the age of 16 years the same period of rest at night which has already been established for women.

The ambassadors of the fourteen European nations are to meet in Berne, Switzerland, in 1914, to take action upon these two proposals.

We cannot participate in this treaty procedure because each of our states is too sovereign to be bound as to its industrial legislation by an international treaty. Yet no state is sovereign enough to bind itself. The action of the European nations in this field is, nevertheless, of immeasurable importance to us. For what seems to them so urgently needful for the health of the working class of all European nations, that they deal with it in this elaborate and comprehensive manner, seems in consequence to the Supreme Court of the

United States to be reasonable when the individual American states enact similar measures. And the Court inclines, therefore, to sustain these measures as constitutional.

At present, only six of our states have established a closing hour at night for the work of women: Massachusetts, New York, Pennsylvania, Connecticut, Indiana and Nebraska. Among these six are, however, the four in which the largest number of women are employed in manufacture.

Four other states—Arizona, California, Colorado and Washington—have established the eight hours day for women and girls, and Oregon has now a working day of eight hours and twenty minutes, and a working week of 50 hours for women of all ages.

In February, 1914, President Wilson signed a bill limiting to eight hours in one day the work of women in industry in the District of Columbia. This applies to virtually all occupations except domestic service, nursing the sick, and office work. The bill was introduced at the request of the National Consumers' League and is the first eight hours law for women in the East.

Industry, Health and Vice

While we thus struggle by petty retail measures against disease, industry produces it by wholesale. If in reply to this it is objected that much illness is due not to work but to personal vices, the use of alcohol and others, the answer is that these, too, are cultivated as a part of the field of industry. The wholesale and retail organization of the alcohol industry has recently forced itself anew upon the attention of the nation by its successful resistance to the enfranchisement of women in Wisconsin, Michigan and Ohio. In all three states there was a well-organized and largely financed campaign of producers and distributors of alcoholic beverages to defeat the suffrage amendments.

The international organization of the white slave traffic is no longer a subject of dispute. Our own government and the governments of European nations are legislating with regard to it.

From these two important disease producing agencies men can free themselves by their own choice. But inescapable accompaniments of industry, perennially producing disease for hundreds of thousands of wage-earners, are fatigue, worry and an insufficient livelihood. Against these the individual is largely powerless.

In April, 1913, the most terrible of all the relations of industry to disease entered upon a unique process of hopeful change. Through the efforts of the voting women of San Francisco, incited originally by an obscure woman worker in the needle trades, Judge Charles Weller was recalled from the Bench. This judge had degraded his high office by systematically protecting men who enticed young girls from honest work into the fields of dishonor. He had reduced the bail of a man under trial charged with being a white slaver. He had protected that incredible American industry—the white slave traffic.

The new voters of San Francisco enlisted enough righteous men to form, with them, a safeguard for wage-earning girls against the most terrible form of exploitation. In doing this they went straight to the root of the most threatening of social diseases, the plague that lurks in undefended girlhood under pressure of underpaid industry. This incident heralds, I believe, a significant approaching change in the relation of industry to health.

III

MODERN INDUSTRY IN RELATION TO EDUCATION

MODERN INDUSTRY AND EDUCATION

We have no national ideal of education, inherited, traditional, corresponding to our ideal of the family. Even the little red school house, with the three R's, meagre symbol of a scant ideal, was never national. It was Northern and Western, as the log school house belonged to the pioneers. The neighborhood school house with a seat for every child, is, in hundreds of counties in the South, still a dream of the future.

We are committed to universal, free, compulsory education of all citizens as the logical corollary of universal suffrage. But the Census of 1910 reveals the fact that we have more than a million and a half native whites, ten years old and older, who are unable to read and write, three per cent. of their number.* Clearly, therefore, we are not at present approaching even the minimum educational achievement demanded of a democratic industrial Republic as the condition of its continued existence.

* 1,535,530 persons, 10 years of age and over, of whom obviously some small per cent. must be presumed to be mentally deficient.

Our ideal of education differs from our ideal of the family in that it is not inherited, but essentially modern. It differs, also, in that we are not falling away from it, as we have fallen away, under the pressure of modern industry, from our ideal of the family, but are approaching it, however slowly.

Throughout this lecture I assume that education is a lifelong process of fitting human beings for life in Society, for self-support, for sharing in the conduct of industry, for parenthood, for the fullest responsibility of citizenship, for all noble enjoyment.

For education in this modern, comprehensive interpretation, industry affords a financial basis and equipment more generous than the human race ever before possessed. Lavishly abundant resources exist for placing instruction at the command of all men, women and children in the Republic. Never was a nation so rich as we are.

The universities number their students by thousands, the elementary schools count their pupils by millions. Yet we are confronted by chronic, wholesale poverty, inextricably associated with gross ignorance. This holds true among native Americans of English stock, in the Southern states, as it does among immigrants in the Northern industrial states. The question thus arises whether poverty and ignorance, in combination, may not be a by-product of modern industry.

When I was in college, students in this country were quite without knowledge of the essential nature of modern industry. At Cornell, where I was a student in 1876, we were taught no economics worthy of the name. At the University of Pennsylvania my brother learned that the point of greatest importance in relation to industry was to understand the theory of a beneficent protective tariff. At Yale our contemporaries were taught by Professor Sumner the supreme advantage of free trade. Later, however, Professor Sumner was the first to awaken in our minds a glimmering consciousness of a permanent wage-earning class in this country by his little volume entitled "What Social Classes Owe to Each Other." Even the courageous pioneer work of Professor Richard T. Ely, at Johns Hopkins, which he has since carried forward there and at the University of Wisconsin, had not then begun. The American faculties of those days cannot be justly blamed for not giving us what they did not possess. Few American teachers of economics and sociology then read French and German. Fewer still had, like Professor Ely, studied in Europe.

The Massachusetts Institute of Technology, Sheffield, Cornell and Lawrence were new, or still in prospect. Training men to apply science in the service of industry was still experimental in the field of higher education, and social science had hardly crossed the Atlantic. The American Social Science Association was not yet a dozen years old.

Then began that application of science in the service of industry which has increasingly absorbed our intellectual ability, and largely deflected it from the task of widening the boundaries of knowledge.

The men whose minds were trained (or left untrained) by the Faculties of those days are the Bench and the Bar, the captains of industry, the Senators and the Faculties of to-day. Men of my generation, and older men, have hitherto decided all things relating to industry and to education, and they are not yet relinquishing that task to their successors. Upon them rests the full responsibility for the anarchical form of industry in the United States in contrast with the beginnings of industrial order visible in some of the European countries. When, in 1883, I was a student of the Faculty of Law in Zurich, professors in Switzerland and Germany were already lecturing on new aspects of industry in courses leading to the degree of Doctor of Laws. In the University of Berlin the same thing was happening. Avowedly impelled by the hope of checking the revolutionary political activity of a rapidly growing party of wage-earners, Prince Bismarck was calling upon the universities to apply to industrial problems the collective wisdom of the leaders of German economic thought; and under his leadership the foundations were laid for that nationwide, inclusive, industrial insurance which the world is now slowly copying.

In my student days we heard much, not only at Cornell, but in the world at large, of the Conflict of Science and Religion. The President of Cornell published volumes on this general theme. But industry, and the laws and courts which bulwarked it, were sacrosanct. They were the Temple and the Ark of the Covenant, and critical study of them would have been blasphemy if anyone had thought of attempting it.

There could not have been a graver misfortune for a great nation in the stage of industrial development in which we then were, than such incompetence in relation to industry as disgraced our American colleges and universities. The wage-earners have ever since been tragically paying the penalty of that default of the higher education, and they must continue to pay until the men of my generation now in control of industry, and of interpreting and enforcing the law in relation to it, shall give way to the new generation. Criticism, however constructive and suggestive, cannot help people who are fifty years old and older to acquire social and industrial vision. The time for that vision is youth. Only the new generation can retrieve our sins of omission and commission, and this they are preparing to do.

Within the academic halls the change amounts to a revolution. Classes in economics and sociology now vie in numbers and popularity with classes in literature. In their brief, sacrificial careers Elizabeth Butler, of Columbia, and Carola Woerishoffer, of Bryn Mawr, heralded the new day that has come, the new challenge that science offers to industry. This old world can never again be quite so sodden when thousands of young men and women are sent forth every year trained to face the world and to strive all their lives to see it exactly as it is.

To these successors we must look for a revolution in education in relation to industry. To them it will not present itself as a revolution, but as a natural next step, when they bring into the foreground of education the teaching of hygiene as applied to every relation of life. For men and women accustomed throughout the high schools, colleges and universities to athletics, to the outdoor life, to physical efficiency, it must seem insanely perverse that we reserve outdoor classes for the children of less and least vitality. For the new generation of educational leaders health will inevitably be the first consideration, in school and in industry. To the new generation we must look, therefore, for the new science that we lack—industrial hygiene—and the new pedagogy that will send forth young workers into industry aware of the provisions which the state enacts for their protection, and alert to avail themselves of the benefits thereof.

One glaring fact confronts the graduates of to-day, namely, the dominant influence of industry in determining the ideals and the administrative policy of our privately endowed universities, colleges and schools, and in modifying the state universities and the public schools. When the graduates leave the universities it is to enter a world in which industry calls a million children a year too early away from the elementary classrooms into its service. It thus creates as its permanent by-product within the voting citizenship illiteracy and stupidity, and broken health bred of monotonous labor.

Enlightening the Consumers

Wholly new within the educational institutions and in the world at large is the attempt to educate the consumers to know and use their power in relation to industry. To-day, more than ever before, the enlightened consumer can truthfully say:

"When I depart this life, I shall have practised certain negative virtues. I shall have done nothing to maintain or encourage certain evil industries. No young girl will have been withdrawn from any class in domestic science to prepare for my use any cigars, cigarettes, chewing gum or tobacco, or rouge, or hairdye, or imitation jewelry. No birds will have been killed to decorate my hats, no children kept at home from kindergarten or primary school, or robbed of their hours of play to 'willow' plumes for my headgear. In these modest abstinences I have striven to keep my individual conscience clear in relation to industry because I, personally, received some education as to the powers of consumers."

Every generous young mind can be kindled to a passionate interest in the relation of working children to itself and its material possessions. And this youthful interest may determine the later activities of a lifetime, as Lord Shaftesbury related that, when he was a lad of fourteen years, the sight of a pauper workingman's funeral modified the whole subsequent course of his life.

How few, however, compared with the whole mass, are the enlightened consumers! How difficult is their path, and how incomplete their present achievement! Why, indeed, is education of consumers left to a volunteer body, such as the Consumers' League?

What help do the rank and file of students in colleges and normal schools get from their Faculties in acquiring this elementary social instruction? Why do not all the colleges inculcate a scientific attitude of mind with regard to industry, awakening the spirit of inquiry, and teaching the available methods of applying this spirit? The colleges have long prepared students for the service of industry. When will they give a like share of attention to the mastery thereof?

A while ago I spoke to the students in a Southern girls' college. They were so young—13 to 19 years or thereabouts—that I asked a member of their Faculty to tell me some of their interests, so that I might connect my suggestions with those interests, as we do with children. She replied, "They don't know anything about anything. They would gladly take an interest, but the President and their mothers don't think they ought to know' much about life." Yet many avenues of approach offered access to those young minds. They were alive to the usefulness of placing early their Christmas orders for candy and chocolates. They responded to an appeal in behalf of overworked young girls in paper-box factories who prepare, at the last moment, boxes for Christmas chocolates and candies, under pressure of "rush orders" of belated shoppers. They saw that daguerreotypes are no longer made because we all prefer photographs, and horsehair sofas are extinct because no one would give them houseroom. And they followed the analogy that goods may be coveted because their history has been righteous throughout the processes of production and distribution. They grasped the suggestion that everything made to-day is made to be sold, that the purchaser is the true Lord of Industry, and that we, all of us, are purchasers. They agreed that there is no longer any innocent bystander.

Even more necessary is such enlightenment in high schools and elementary schools. In certain practical ways it can be begun very early. Thus the Paulist Fathers in New York City have, for years, through their Sunday School, appealed to children, even little ones, and their mothers, to be considerate about Christmas shopping. And nuns of teaching orders, during one of their summer schools on the Pacific Coast, listened receptively to an officer of the Consumers' League explaining to them the possibility of similar suggestions to their pupils.

The children in grammar grades, and still more those in high schools, are keenly alert to suggestions of the power we all potentially possess as consumers. Their interest in regard to things that they buy is of the liveliest. They are in nowise blasé. Beginning with their hair ribbons, tracing them back to the silk mills in New Jersey and Pennsylvania, school girls care eagerly to know why, in silk ribbon mills, wages are low, and work-rooms hot and stuffy, and how it comes that quick, capable girls, hardly older than themselves, must serve as pacemakers for slower and less gifted workers.

Any restless school boy, at the hobbledehoy age, will listen to the story of the "grinders' phthisis" that cuts down in their prime men who prepare blades for pocket-knives; to a description of need-less danger to other boys arising from unguarded machines in pencil factories, and of the small pay that goes with putting rubbers in pencils. Tales of mine and breaker boys and young lads working at night in glass works in West Virginia find a responsive chord in the breasts of school boys, who readily see that none of us escape using coal and glass. They, too, perceive that there are, in this case, no innocent bystanders, that we are all tarred with the same stick.

Working-class children during their few brief years in the elementary schools need the appeal to sympathetic imagination the more because of the dulling experience that befalls them in the long years of work that follow. Their direst need is for cultivation of their critical sense in relation to industry.

Refreshing is the alert response of young minds stirred by the idea of their relation, previously an unconscious one, as indirect employers. Curiously varied is the expression of the faces of a high school class when asked how they account for the fact, by no means inevitable, that other children of their own age are less educated than themselves? They are visibly shocked by a blunt statement that the present difference in opportunity is due not to their own superior gifts, or to the superior thrift or generosity, necessarily, of their parents, but to the defective organization of education and of industry. To most young minds the idea is fascinatingly new that the transformation of industry is to-day the life and death question of this Republic.

This new education of youth the Nation sorely needs. We must establish in *all* the oncoming generation an unwearying spirit of inquiry with regard to industry. Nothing can safely be assumed in relation to it. Is it paying its social costs? Is its product, indeed, value received? Does it bring forth beauty? Or does it give us personal adornment at cost of smoke-laden, filthy sky and air?

Child Labor

Far, however, from educating the children of wage-earners to intelligent criticism as consumers, the schools surrender them too early to the service of industry, and tend increasingly to rob the few years now sacred to childhood by making the schools' work vocational and industrial. The new vocational effort largely addresses itself to fitting American youth to escape from machine tending, to become foremen, managers, superintendents. But in the nature of industry the opportunities for such work are a trivial fraction of the whole. Vast multitudes must be machine tenders, and machines increase daily, and under the present conditions machines destroy mind.

For more than a century philanthropists have struggled in England and, more recently, in this country, to safeguard children of wage earners from destruction by industry. The National Child Labor Committee, the National Consumers' League, the National Education Association, and other national bodies galore have for years worked to assure educational opportunity to all the children. They strive to establish minimum standards below which the school year may not be shortened, children may not leave school unable to read and write, and industrial employment may be forbidden.

Always and everywhere they find the same forces opposing them. Rural industries claim children for the beet fields, the cotton and tobacco fields, the bean and pea fields, the berry patches, the cranberry bogs, the canneries, and the orchards. Coal mines consume boys in breakers and underground. Urban industries, too, cotton and woollen and silk mills, glass works, sweatshops, the messenger service, and the newspapers, all industries—the world over—in which children can be employed, are forever calling them from school to work.

Only the men and women who are engaged in the struggle year after year know how powerful and how active are the interests that profit by the labor of children. In four Southern states—the Carolinas, Georgia and Alabama—the cotton mill interest has hitherto succeeded in preventing the adoption of the fourteenth birthday as the lowest limit for children beginning to work. In West Virginia the glass companies and the mine owners killed all child labor legislation at the session of 1913. In Pennsylvania in the same year the glass companies and the textile manufacturers successfully made common cause against the working children, killed the child labor bill, and

kept in force the old law. Under it boys of fourteen years may still be legally required to work
eight hours at night in glassworks and all other
industries having continuing processes.

Children have a statutory limit of their working day to eight hours in twenty-four in only one
Southern state, Mississippi, and in only one New
England state, Massachusetts. Forty states now
forbid employment of children before the fourteenth birthday. Only the Southern cotton manufacturing states show no disposition thus to protect their young boys and girls and give them
time for a rudimentary education. Of children
who work on these terms, what cant it is to say
that they have "a square deal," or "an equal opportunity" with children of the socialized Northwestern states, with their long childhood safe-
guarded from wage-earning, with abundant
schools, and free university tuition to tempt them
to continue the process of education!

For the unfortunate children, twelve and thirteen years old, of the belated Southern cotton
manufacturing states, the federal bill pending before Congress seems to offer new hope. It rein-
troduces the idea of federal action in defence of
boys and girls now legally employed below the age
of fourteen years in mills and mines. It proposes
to exclude from interstate commerce all goods

derived from mills or mines in which children below the age of fourteen years are employed.

The federal bill thus brings into sharp relief the fact that native white orphans, of native parentage, in Georgia are future citizens of this Republic as surely as the happier immigrant children of New York, or the native children of the enlightened and humane Northwestern states. As future citizens, the children of the South need fourteen years, at least, of childhood in which to grow and learn. And the bill appeals to the whole nation to see that this claim is enforced, this right is guaranteed to them.

The Working Class Children

Modern industry tends to keep the wage-earners spiritually poor and dull. Of all the charges made against it to-day this is the gravest. The ultimate blasphemy is the proposal to fit children for industry as industry is. It must be revolutionized before it will be fit for children and youth to enter. It must first be made democratic and cooperative, transformed into service.

The need of to-day is for education to enable children and youth, and men and women, to resist the ruinous, stupefying influence of industry. To make this resistance successful, the schools must keep the whole body of young workers on their rolls at least for regular part time attendance, until the twenty-first birthday, until the education *for* citizenship ends, and education *by and through* the duties of citizenship begins. One short step in this direction has been taken in Wisconsin and in Ohio, where the working week of children below the 16th birthday is reduced to 48 hours, of which five must be spent in continuous classes. Enlightened teachers of these classes strive to rekindle in working boys and girls, from week to week, the intellectual life which industry tends to extinguish by dulling monotonous work. This is one line of hopeful effort in a direction immeasurably important, for in a Republic on pain of utter failure the common laborers must be educated citizens. Massachusetts has for many years recognized this, at least in a modest degree, in the statute which holds the employer responsible for regular school attendance of all illiterate minor employés.

In speaking to teachers about vocational training, my one appeal to them is to fit every child to resist the pressure of industry, to inculcate in all children the ambition to become cooperative citizens, keeping themselves in health, practising the art of thinking. Above all else is the need to cherish their critical faculty, to train them to resist monotony, and to organize their own activities for themselves, so that they may combat successfully the deadliest foe of this Republic, the lowering of the citizenship by industry. How else can the wage workers regain their lost share of control and develop anew the sense of civic and industrial responsibility?

Far from equipping children to maintain themselves against its injurious tendencies, our elementary schools tend rather to serve as feeders for industry. Domestic science begins commonly in the sixth or seventh grade, if at all, while daughters of working families leave by thousands from the fifth to enter upon industrial life. When a little immigrant girl fresh from the steerage enters school in the foreign colony of a manufacturing city, she makes on the first day the acquaintance of Teacher, who is thenceforth her ideal lady. Teacher is usually young, friendly, dressed in shirtwaist, necktie, trig skirt, belt, and shoes with heels. She catches the little girl's imagination, and a process of imitation begins which lasts at least until the child's 14th birthday. But throughout all that time, never once does Teacher do anything which Mother is seen to do at home. If the windows are ever washed, it is by the janitor or his assistant, and usually out of school hours. If the floor is scrubbed, the process is unseen. Washing day is unknown within the classroom, and babies are alien to the activities of Teacher. Not so much as a cup of cocoa or a slice of toast is she seen to prepare by any girl who leaves from the "working paper grades."

By their one-sided curriculum, the schools may truthfully be said actively to divert the little daughters of wage-earning families from home life to becoming cash girls and factory hands. For the schools teach exactly those things which prepare girls to become at the earliest moment cash children and machine tenders: punctuality, regularity, attention, obedience, and a little reading and writing—excellent things in themselves, but wretched preparation either for domestic service as an alternative choice of occupations, or for homemaking a decade later on in the lives of the pupils.

With our material supplies in lavish abundance for the full and generous education of every man, woman and child throughout this whole country, our trouble is our own lack of vision, in city, state and nation.

Teaching is already a public service, although the ethics of Boards of Education are still largely commercial, because these Boards are chiefly composed of business men, with an occasional physician whose ideals vary but slightly from theirs. The teaching staff itself, being in contact with

the children, is increasingly socially minded. But
the teaching staff, also, is vitiated by sordid ideals
derived from its competitive environment.   It,
too, suffers the taint of modern industry.

Where the National Child Labor Committee,
when it entered the field ten years ago, reasonably expected to find its strongest allies, among
principals and teachers, it has found, in a disap-
pointing number of individual cases, an unthink-
ing willingness to surrender children—under pre-
text of their poverty—to the greedy hunger of
mills, mines, sweatshops, cotton fields, and the
city street trades. Many children leave school by
reason of the perverse suggestions of their teachers.

Not from the teaching staff has come the in-
sistent demand for scholarships to keep *all* the
children in school at least to the 16th birthday.

Surely our grandchildren will look back with
wonder that we, who waste money in war and
preparations for war, leave 80,000 children permanently in half-time classes for want of school room
in the greatest industrial city in this hemisphere,
and issue in New York City in one year 42,000
working papers to children below the age of 16
years.   The records of illiterate children ten to
fourteen years old form a part of every decennial
federal Census, chiefly of native children of native

parents, in the Southern states. We let boys and girls go into monotonous occupations at fourteen years old or earlier, before their judgment has had time to develop. Yet industry holds out to the rank and file of those who leave from the fifth and sixth grades—the educational steerage—little hope of orderly promotion such as they have experienced in school, and slight promise of later variety of employment, or material increase in wages.

All this with no resounding protest from the teaching staff! Small wonder that the children lack the instruction adapted to prepare them for the change from our industrial chaos to the orderly industrial service of the future!

Unacquainted with industry and out of touch with it, untrained in the principles and practice of cooperation, disfranchised and thus deprived of the education derived from active citizenship, the teachers of our schools are, in most of the states, failing the children to-day, as the universities and colleges failed their students in the Nineteenth Century. They are not educating the masses of children to be masters of industry. On the contrary, they are participating—at least to the extent of passive acquiescence—in the evil process of making them slaves of machines.

What sixth grade class in this whole nation

sends out its pupils fortified with full knowledge of the meagre laws framed for their protection? What children are taught in school that they cannot before the 16th birthday legally work in New York after five o'clock in a factory, and after seven in a store? How many know that they are entitled to seats with backs and to the use thereof whenever the nature of their work permits such use? Is there anything that they more urgently need to know than these eminently practical items? But how many teachers know even these few things about industry as it is to-day? And how can they teach what they do not know?

How many normal schools require their graduating classes to pass an examination in the provisions of the compulsory education law, and the labor law applying to children and adolescents? But without this knowledge, how can the graduates, when they find positions, be sure of obeying the statutes themselves? And how can they instruct their "working paper classes" and other appropriate grades as to the protection which the law provides and the children are entitled to claim in factories, stores and workshops?

Machine Tenders

Modern industry calls increasingly for common labor not only to dig with pick and shovel, but to do a thousand simplified things for which young hands, fourteen to sixteen years old, being obtainable for low wages, are commercially preferred to the hands of older persons. Requiring attention, speed and some slight dexterity but no other quality, such work deadens young minds. Machine tending habituates them to irresponsibility and monotony, to the utter absence of thought, of inventiveness, of judgment, of ambition. Men and women who have spent these plastic years in this way are worse human beings, not better ones, for their contact with industry.

Obviously machine tending fits no girl for bringing up children in a home of her own later on, or for taking any part whatever in domestic life. The special skill that she needs as future wife and mother is skill in the art of living. Prolonged machine tending prepares no boy for promotion to the post of foreman or superintendent. On the contrary, the longer a boy tends a machine, the less is he likely to develop qualities fitting him for managing men or affairs. In the words of Joseph Lee, of Boston, president of the National Playgrounds Association of America, such employment *dis*educates growing minds.

Work must be done, however. Obviously, it must not be done by young children, or in large measure by adolescents. Who shall do it in order that the least injury may be wrought? What does machine tending do to older minds? Many years ago when I was chief factory inspector of the State of Illinois, I found, in a tin can factory, a shelf filled with young boys whose duty was to watch unceasingly a never-ending procession of lids of tomato cans, milk cans, soup cans, cans for all sorts of goods, as these lids came down a slit in an incline from the upper to the lower floor. When a can lid was defective, a boy picked it out. Small fingers were cut and tied up in rags. Young legs and backs were made crooked, young eyes were strained by continuous watching. The work was legal, once the boys were 14 years old and had filed employment certificates at the factory office; but young minds and bodies were cramped, stupefied and deadened in that work. I asked Mr. Henry Demarest Lloyd to go with me to see those boys, hoping that he might make them the text of some noble chapter, perhaps in his volume on the Lords of Industry.

On the way to them he saw a man, white-haired like himself, watching an endless procession of cans to which the lids would later be attached. This work called for no quality of mind, but sustained attention to a horrible monotony. The man watched perpetually for dents in tin cans, and when a can was dented, he removed it, using one hand at long intervals. He needed good sight in order never to miss a dent. Thirteen years he had sat there, day after day, looking at cans. Millions of them had passed before his eyes and gone their ways to the dump after their brief service was rendered. His industrial usefulness was reduced to the use of his eyes exclusively. If they should lose their keenness, he would be a pauper. For discovering dents in cans is not work that society recompenses with a margin for savings.

To Mr. Lloyd, then at the height of his powers, those lost thirteen years were a tragedy. He was fascinated, horrified at the sight of the slave of the machine. The man was a native American, educated to read and write, but at the end of ten hours' work his eyes were too weary for reading. All his powers were absorbed by seeking dents in cans; whatever intelligence he exercised, he had to summon after exhausting the day's normal supply of power of attention.

That can-watcher is a type of millions of men who, in an infinite variety of ways, are reduced to some one form of attention. Often that is the sole demand upon one, his other powers atrophy by disuse. But the permanent tendency of industry is to install more automatic machines, to require more tenders, perhaps one for one machine, perhaps one for six, or eight, or twenty. And their inevitable tendency is to make the machine tender automatic like themselves. All intelligence for the performance of a voter's duty the machine tender must get and keep in spite of his work.

For this more, perhaps, than for any other reason, the working day in industry must be shortened for men as well as for women and youth, to save human faculties from being utterly deadened in the modern process of production, and to afford leisure for the valuable active uses of the mind. The unskilled laborer's working day must be shortened, his wage assured, the tasks of self-government laid upon him, not only as a citizen, but in his industry. This the trade unions have insisted upon for two generations. But the courts have not yet sustained *on these grounds* any statute limiting the hours of labor of men or women.

The courts hold that, where obvious physical injury results from excessive hours of work, the freedom of contract may be abridged. But courts and legislators do not see that an industry which by long daily hours of monotonous work dulls the mind of the voters, attacks the life of the Republic. It has, so far as I know, never been held that working hours can be shortened by statute in the interest of the public intelligence.

Had the educated men of my generation been

trained in youth to insight and vision, to discern
the industrial process of stupefying and, on the
other hand, the demand of expanding democracy
for intelligence in all the citizens, how different
must have been their recent attitude toward the
movement for a shorter working day, for one
day's rest in seven, for the abolition of night work
in every possible case!

Democracy makes ever-widening demands upon
the time and intelligence of the citizens. The initiative and referendum, the recall, proportional
voting, direct primaries—the new processes of
democracy—call into action growing bodies of
public-spirited citizens, and demand of the rank
and file a continuing series of decisions on matters
of importance. Workmen's compensation, minimum wage boards, mothers' pensions, the short
working day, child labor, compulsory education,
equal suffrage, are all being legislated upon. Several of these measures call for popular votes, and
all of them concern wage-earning people. There
is incessant call for more intelligence in the voting
constituency. But what intelligence can a man
or woman exercise whose mind is dimmed by
spending ten hours or more every day watching
for dents in cans? How can weary eyes and a
jaded mind be used for thoughtful reading on political subjects? What is left wherewith to make

decisions?   It is an irreconcilable conflict of experience.

The Wage Earners Educating Themselves

Men and women employed in monotonous industries in this country have missed the stimulus and education derived by cooperators from their personal interest in their cooperative business, because they have shirked the task of cooperative production and distribution carried forward on a vast scale during the past half century in England and on the Continent.   In England one in six of the adult population is a cooperator, and wage-earning consumers sharing in the control of production and distribution acquire admirable social education in the process.   All this has been lost out of the experience of American wage earners.   Cooperative industry calls for sustained intelligent effort by *all* the cooperators.   Public ownership calls for an intelligently critical voting constituency forever alert to public affairs.   But how can these qualities be demanded of common laborers, of machine tenders, of men and women speeded as American industry drives them today?

Chief among the agencies of education, for good or evil, is work.   The twin sources of human character which have fitted the race for civilization

are the daily work done since the race began, and
the discipline derived from family life since the
first human mother cradled her first child. The
schools awaken intelligence in multitudes of children during the few years of childhood, but the
character and the intellectual development of the
nations are determined by the long, unending discipline of work.

Our gravest mistake is habitually considering
education as an experience of youth; worse still,
as a process of preparing children for industry.
While consciousness remains, life itself is educating us.

An illuminating little book, a creative study of
one of our lost opportunities for making industry
the handmaiden of education is unhappily con-
cealed and disguised by its author, Gerald Stan-
ley Lee, under the silly title, "Inspired Million-
aires." It has substantial merit; it presents
vividly the stimulating effect upon mill hands
which would follow if they moved step by step,
in regular promotion, from one part of the work
of the mill to another so that in an industrial lifetime all the employés might come into contact
with every process for which they are not physically or mentally incapacitated.

Whenever the workers with hand and brain
grasp the possibilities that lurk in this idea, they

will undoubtedly make it the complement to the present sordid "efficiency" movement. Their goal will be the efficiency of the manual worker as a human being, not merely his efficiency in producing goods as means to profits. Then no man will be reduced, like the slave of tin cans, to the use of his eyes alone. In that man's work there was never the waste of a motion: there was only the waste of a human life.

In a near-by university city, which is also a manufacturing centre, I spoke recently to an audience of about four hundred wage-earning men and women. We were in a loathsome little hall, used during the week for moving picture shows, for the cruel waste of the school buildings, unused at night, entails the cost of rent upon wage earners who would gladly use schools as they now use the ugly, ill-ventilated premises which alone their wages can command. The air was poisonously bad, but the audience remained from eight to eleven on Sunday evening, discussing the prosaic subject of minimum wages boards. Their eager, sustained attention was wonderful and, at the end of my hour-long monologue, they asked questions. I know much more about minimum wages boards from defending them under that hail of penetrating questions. They had looked eagerly forward through the week to Sunday, preparing those

questions. Despite the bad air, they had succeeded in listening critically. For them any possible change in industrial conditions, however minor
they may think that change likely to prove under
the test of experience, kindles the mind. They
are people under stress.

This is one of the most vital processes of education going forward to-day—this deliberate, continuing effort of men and women, many of them
already disciplined by experience in labor unions,
to brace themselves against the destructive pressure of industry; to regain for themselves and
their fellow wage earners some share of possession
and control of industry, through cooperation,
through public ownership, through every possible
extension of democracy.

Thousands of such groups of working men and
women are, throughout their long hours of
monotony in the week, saving their minds from
utter ruin by pondering the themes which they
discuss in their meetings on Sunday. Scattered
everywhere throughout the nation, they are safeguarding their health and intelligence, and developing their morals and citizenship. In spite of
their stupefying work, and with cruelly little help
from the constituted educational authorities, the
wage earners are educating themselves.

IV

MODERN INDUSTRY IN RELATION TO MORALITY

MODERN INDUSTRY AND MORALITY

We are undergoing a transition in the life of the nation greater than any hitherto experienced, a change immeasurably greater than the freeing of four million slaves, a half century ago, as an incident of a long and terrible war. This transition is of such import that it is quite impossible for us in the midst of it to measure its scope. Whether or not we are aware of it, whether we like it or not, we are living in the initial stages of the change from work done almost universally for private gain to work in the service of all.

The vast multitude of federal employés who conduct the postal service, the health service, the forestry service, are soon to be augmented by railway and telegraph workers administering public transportation and communication. Postmaster-General Hitchcock, after introducing parcels posts and postal banks, left, as his parting message to the American people, advice that the public should own the telegraphs and telephones, and several cities in North Dakota are already taking his ad-

113

vice.* Postal savings banks and the parcels post
came to us long after Europe had tested them,
and only when our need was so urgent that they
could not longer be deferred, and then only when
the national banks were assured the privilege of
receiving the postal bank deposits at two per cent.
They are now a matter of course.

Vast reclamation schemes applying to swamp
and desert lands, and river regulation on a scale
previously undreamed of, are already carried out,
or are now in process, or are definitely planned by
the federal authorities; and Congress is never
without measures under consideration looking in
these directions.

Mr. Stimson, Secretary of War under Mr. Taft,
made vigorous recommendations for federal activities in relation to water storage and the use of
power generated from navigable rivers, and the
floods have given new weight to his words. The
Secretary of the Navy has made public facts
which strongly support the bill pending in Congress for establishing public armor plate works for
the use of the Navy.

The physical valuation of the railways by the
Interstate Commerce Commission, a long and ex-
ceedingly difficult step toward public ownership,

---

* Postmaster-General Burleson is bringing the proposal actively forward in the Wilson administration.

is already under way. And an appropriation for building a federal railroad in Alaska is in force.

Ever-widening areas of industry are coming into public possession, to be administered by cities, states and by the federal government: education, elementary and advanced, the public library business, lighting, the provision of milk, water, ice and coal, the use of water power for generating electricity, as in the great hydro-electric works at Lewiston, Maine, and Houston, Texas.*

* Among items too numerous to catalogue the following are current:—

Seattle owns a street car line, and San Francisco both owns and operates one; Detroit and Cleveland have voted to acquire car lines. Boston and New York City own subways, though the citizens of New York have cause for bitter regret that theirs is leased to private corporations.

Three Southern cities—two in Texas and one in Tennessee —own municipal abattoirs, and the federal Department of Agriculture vigorously recommends that all cities establish them. City health inspectors are as much a matter of course as the police, and are now reinforced by school nurses and doctors, while municipal physicians and nurses in the tuberculosis service, the maternity service, and the hospital follow-up work are increasing even more rapidly than are city milk stations. Serums and vaccines are commonly furnished by public health authorities.

It has recently been held by the Supreme Court of Georgia that the city of Camilla may make and sell ice, and New York City is now establishing a municipal ice plant. Schenectady buys and sells ice and coal in the service of its citizens. Philadelphia has been sustained by the Pennsylvania courts

The transition from competition to public service is far advanced. The very recent change in attitude of legislatures and courts is more significant than the actual tasks already undertaken.

The material conditions for the vast change are at hand, and many phases of the transition have already been successfully achieved in other countries whose experience awaits our study.

The coming public service will test our morality on the largest scale yet applied to it. Can our democracy administer industry? Have we, as a nation, the moral qualities requisite for enduring that moral strain?

We who are here, living in the midst of the transition, make our contribution to it consciously or unconsciously. We shape it, determine its character, and we are ill-fitted for the task. We suffer the disadvantage of living in a period when the morality of our great-grandparents is outgrown, and that of our grandchildren is not yet established. We live in a period of disintegration, of unparallelled moral pressure, and inadequate moral guidance, with the duty resting upon us of

in its policy of buying land in excess of its immediate needs in connection with a boulevard.

The state of Wisconsin leases land in its lake region to summer tenants. It also sells insurance; and savings bank insurance in Massachusetts is increasingly a state affair.

scanning the horizon for every ray which may serve to illumine and guide us.

The fundamental moral teaching that prevailed on this continent when the Republic was founded had its roots in the experience of an agricultural people—its precepts and maxims were in harmony with and adequate to the clear demands of responsibility and decency within the rural family. Those precepts defined the duties of father, mother and children living upon the farm which they owned and controlled, from which they derived their subsistence—a self-sustaining group— and the simple relations of such a family group with other similar family groups. Complex modern industrial relations did not develop until the middle of the Nineteenth Century. Then came, after the Civil War, the change *crescendo* to the full complexity in which we live.

To-day agriculture is still our chief industry, despite the modern development which has made us the most industrially productive of all nations; and the morality of agricultural individualism is our accepted morality. This affords no adequate guidance in the intricate relations of our rapidly changing life; and its insufficiency becomes from year to year more obvious with the evolution of industry. Between that obsolete morality which remains embodied in our laws, and our human needs in modern daily life, the contradiction has become intolerable.

It is ominous that the industrial change comes not because the American people are intellectually convinced that it is desirable, but because past conditions can no longer be endured. It is, for instance, not reassuring that we are being driven toward public ownership of railroads by the incompetence and dishonesty of private management, and the consequent sacrifice of life, limb, health and welfare of employés and of travellers.

This is, however, the case at the present moment. Over-capitalization, insufficient equipment, overworked employés, appalling railway accidents, belated travel, delayed freight—these accompaniments of irresponsible anonymous ownership are driving conservative New England toward responsible public ownership of her railroads. Meanwhile the Panama railroad offers an enticing sample on a small scale of the ability of the federal government to administer transportation, even under present difficulties.

Irresponsible Anonymous Ownership

The old theory was that enlightened self-interest could be trusted to conduct industry, that the sum of all selfish interests would coincide with public interest. Tested in practice, however, this theory has not sustained modern life. Industry conducted for profit and regulated only by the pressure of competition (the labor being performed by men, women and children who are merely "hands") has produced, among its fruits, the maximum cynical disregard of the manhood, womanhood and childhood of the workers, and a loss of moral responsibility in the relation of the owners of industry to the consuming public.

The fundamental immorality of our era from which innumerable smaller ills arise is that the worker has lost the ownership and control of his tools, his means of production. In the evolution from the distaff and spinning wheel to the cotton mill village owned anonymously by bond and stockholders who may live in Europe, or in South America, or Japan, the old foundation of industrial morality, honesty between two individual persons, is no longer adequate.

The modern wage worker deprived of ownership and control of his tools is not obviously dependent like the chattel slave before` the emancipation, or the coolie before the exclusion laws, or the peon, whom the federal government still occasionally discovers in the South, where at this moment peonage exists, in horrifying forms, in the mining regions in West Virginia. The great mass of wage-earning people are not now consciously dependent as the Negroes and Chinese were. They are not like them conspicuously in need of being freed by the federal authorities.

The fundamental immorality to-day is far more subtle. Instead of the wage earners owning and thereby controlling things, as the farmers did in the agricultural period, they are now under the control of things (products and means of production). Through those things they are controlled by other human beings who, as stockholders and bond owners, possess perhaps a great factory town like Gary, Indiana, or a cotton mill village in Rhode Island or Georgia—a modern Frankenstein into which the ancient tools of the workers have now developed.

As an example of such anonymous, impersonal ownership, I venture once more to refer to the former conditions in the steel industry, to the cruelty, among others, of excessive working hours in intolerable heat. When in the Pittsburgh Survey the exact facts were made public, Mr. Charles Cabot, a stockholder in the steel industry, protested that these things were not and, in the nature of things, could not be true. When, however, the statements had all been substantiated, Mr. Cabot declared that every shareholder in that industry ought to know these conditions. He, therefore, asked the corporation for a list of stock-

holders in order that he might bring the facts to
the knowledge of the owners, his fellow bond and
stockholders in the industry. Three years passed
before he succeeded in getting the list.

In a great corporation owned by bond and
stockholders nobody knows who is the employer.
The employer is a vast composite changing from
day to day with every transfer of stocks and
bonds. Nor are the employés known. Even the
manager or foreman often knows a given employé
only as a number on the pay roll. If the "hand"
is killed, buried, perhaps, in molten metal, nobody knows who has perished except from the
number on his locker. So entirely anonymous is
the relation between stockholder and employé,
and among fellow owners in the most highly developed of our industries. This form, this organization of industry, and this anonymous relation
within it, have grown up since the Civil War.
The steel industry is, perhaps, the perfect example
of the alienation of the anonymous worker and
anonymous employer. It is the current industrial
ideal of organization toward which the great industries tend—the uttermost detachment of the
worker from ownership of the tools, and utter
freedom on the part of the owners from personal
responsibility alike toward the workers and the
community.

One incidental result of this detachment is a lack of scruple on the part of the anonymous owners of a given industry, the employers of the labor engaged in it, toward the consuming public. One of the earliest maxims laid down for the guidance of people entering trade is the old Roman saying: *Caveat emptor*—Let the purchaser beware! Never was it more applicable than to-day. The anonymous relation of the person offering goods for sale is fundamentally immoral primarily because it is devoid of responsibility.

The federal pure food act proclaims to the world that our food-producing industries, although they are organized with greater ability than has ever before been devoted to the task, cannot be trusted to feed America. The meat inspection law publishes similar tidings of the meat industry to the people who consume its product.

When federal inspection of the stock yards was forced upon us by the German government, which excluded from German territory our meat products unless the commercial integrity of the packers and the purity of their goods were guaranteed by the federal government, the brand upon the meat incidentally branded the packers. The morality of the men in charge of this great staple American industry has never borne any proportion to their ability. Yet the federal Department of Agriculture for years permitted the sale to us of meat which could not be guaranteed by it and, therefore, could not be sent abroad. These things have been possible because the ownership of the vast and complicated meat industry had been irresponsible. There is no moral restraint on the part of managers of stock yards. Theirs is a property, an investment, not a service.

A similar thing was true long ago of the Scotch fisheries. The contents of the kegs of herring were notoriously different from their labels, so that foreign consumers demanded as a guarantee of honest contents the brand of the English government. Most products are, however, not sold to foreign nations able to establish and to enforce upon us an international standard of integrity. The slow passage of the pure-food law by Congress (requiring eighteen years of continuous effort) and the painful, largely unsuccessful struggle to get the law enforced against powerful food-producing companies and their agents in the press, indicate the patience of the American people in the presence of commercial dishonesty and lack of standards.

The public accepts with heartfelt admiration gifts to charity and to the higher education from known adulterators of food, so confused are our moral standards in relation to industry. And this confusion is a normal product of modern industry.

One sinister consequence of the anonymous, impersonal ownership of business, and the accompanying degradation of the workers to the position of "hands," is their own acceptance of this position. Filthy or diseased meat, adulterated eatables, short-weight packages, though the product of their labor appear to them to be no concern of theirs. They feel no share in the guilt of the employing concern under whose orders, and in whose pay, they put alum in bread, formaldehyde in milk, tin, lead or iron in silk (in the process of dyeing), or shoddy in place of wool in garments to be worn by other working people. Steel workers know when there are blow holes in armor plates, but they regard it as no affair of theirs. The negotiation is between the steel manufacturer and the Navy Department, and the wage earner's experience has awakened in him no patriot's rage against such treason. If he thinks at all of the matter, it is perhaps to reflect that wars are fought to the profit of financiers, and at cost of working people, whichever side wins. Or the steel worker may sullenly remember that he has long been begging the Government to abolish contract work and make its own steel plate.

In any case, the irresponsible state of mind of employing corporations and indifferent "hands" is more threatening to civilization than the actual harm inflicted by alum, formaldehyde, shoddy, blow holes and all the other poisons and dishonest products. And this indifference, like the moral confusion of the general public concerning gifts derived from these and similar sinister sources for the higher education, philanthropy and religion, is a normal product of modern industry.

Our confusion is well illustrated in relation to our concept of murder.

The Old Commandment in the New Order

The Commandment, Thou Shalt Not Kill, is still valid in our laws to the extent that the individual murderer of an individual person pays with his life for his crime, the hangman or electrocutioner being held—somewhat whimsically—exempt from the effect of the Commandment. But wholesale killing in industry as in war remains unpunished.

Our morality has been sapped by precept and practice, by living in a society in which the moral foundations of industry are false and corrupting. The human mind accepts without revolt that to which it is accustomed from childhood. Cannibals were not horrified at eating their grandparents. Soldiers do not recoil from murder, they plan it systematically years in advance; and on the field of battle they bayonet men as butchers stick pigs. And gentle grandmothers give little children paper or tin soldiers as playthings, and read of bayonet charges with enthusiasm.

Owners of tenement houses do not count themselves infanticides, though the death rate of babies in tenements is twice as large as elsewhere. On the contrary, the real estate interests fight as one man every requirement of tenement house sanitation which seems to threaten to cut into their incomes. The landlords' resistance to improved housing is uninterrupted and nation wide.

Although dirty milk is a permanently active cause of disease and death, the milk producers and dealers succeeded in 1913 in defeating legislation calculated to assure greater cleanliness in the rural treatment of the milk supply of New York City.

Builders, managers, stock and bond holders of factories are not punished as murderers, though a hundred and more men and women perish by fire and smoke in a single work room. In connection with the most terrible of factory fires, the owners of the building have been absolved by the courts of New York State from all criminal responsibility for the monstrous slaughter, and the firm is still doing business.

When hundreds of women and children on a Sunday School outing in the East River perished by drowning, many of the victims were lost because the cork safety belts carried on the boat were weighted with lead or iron, substances cheaper than cork in belts bought and sold by weight. Only the captain of the Slocum was punished. Manufacturers and dealers in cork safety belts appear to be free to continue to furnish their death-dealing wares.

We are by way of forgetting the Iroquois Theatre in Chicago in which children were suffocated at a matinée. The manager—far from having been punished for failing to supply the needed precautions for safety—appeared before a legislative committee at Springfield, in 1911, insolently to oppose, and demand the repeal of, the beneficent Illinois statute which keeps young children off the stage.

Some years ago a speculator cornered the ice supply in summer in New York City. The price rose, poor mothers could not buy ice, and the list of deaths of babies lengthened, for milk without ice is poison in the tenements in summer. Later for an offence unrelated to this, the speculator was sent to a federal penitentiary for a long term. Upon the representations of reputable physicians that the convict was about to die, the President

pardoned him. Our moral sense is dulled by
modern industry, and the President in pardon-
ing a single influential one among hundreds
of sick convicts, and one whose record was,
perhaps, the most anti-social of all, did but act in
accordance with prevailing standards.

It is silly and confusing to tilt at Big Business,
as though bigness in itself were the sole or the
chief active element in our political and industrial
immorality. The pushcart peddlers and news ven-
dors who have stands on city street corners are
animated by precisely the same business motives
as the gas trust, the surface car companies and all
the other large exploiters of the cities. And their
very numbers make the little offenders perhaps
the more insidiously poisonous to the community,
in these days of transition to new forms of industry calling for new and loftier morality. The
source of corruption in large and small alike is irresponsibility, the relation to the community of
freebooting exploiters in a society which sends
those who fail to the almshouse and the potter's
field.

Morally Extra Hazardous Employments

In any review of the moral aspects of our present transition, our failure to develop voluntary
cooperation in distribution looms large. We are

punished for our sins of omission by having the vastest department store industry in the world with its morally extra hazardous employment of thousands of underpaid, inexperienced young women and girls, transferred from the meagre life of the tenement and the narrow, rigid routine of the elementary school to the midst of luxury such as had not been invented in the days of Louis XVI. In the midst of this poisonous luxury they are paid from three dollars a week upward.

In the interest of the public morals—because of the nature of the surroundings and the unlimited access of the public—the demand would be a legitimate one that girls should not be employed in department stores before the 21st birthday, until their youthful character had time to solidify.

The investment in department stores is stupendous. In the whole country it runs into hundreds of millions, upon which dividends must be earned. Window dressing, counter dressing, and newspaper advertising are obviously directed to the single purpose of enticing consumers, chiefly women, to buy, in addition to the necessary staples, articles of which they would otherwise not think. Its aim is the enticement of consumers, as adulterating goods in manufacture is intended to exploit them.

This particular form of moral strain was unknown before the present half century. The disproportion between what the employés get and what surrounds them, indicates the cynicism, the blunted sympathy of the consuming public. Were women richer in discernment, in sympathetic imagination, we must have registered long since our veto upon this *mis*education of ourselves and of those who serve us in the stores. As an index both of our undeveloped sympathy and of our potential power as consumers, these stores are monumental. We have never even discerned how pernicious is their influence in the great cities.

Had we developed a cooperative movement in proportion to our retail distribution, comparable to the similar movements in England, Germany and Belgium, our exploitation of young workers in retail trade could never have reached its present extent. In cooperative commerce there is virtually no advertising. Goods are made, transported and sold to meet human needs which require no stimulation. The consequent saving to the public is not confined to dollars and cents. For both employés and purchasers the saving of moral strain is incalculable.

How alien to our whole habit of mind is the demand for an administration of industry giving to the workers active benefit throughout the process of work itself! We may, indeed, be justly charged with having maintained a national policy of pressure upon the wage earners. For generations we imported slaves. When that form of competition was abolished, there came the coolies. After their Irish competitors succeeded in getting them excluded, peonage and child labor loomed up, and still exist. Now the steerage brings detached young girls by tens of thousands from Europe.

Every immigrant girl who enters upon manufacture or commerce is a living threat to the standard of life of men and women already here. Witness Lawrence, Little Falls, the stockyards, the underpaid needle trades, the department stores.

Since the Children's Crusade, dark episode of the Dark Ages, there has been no international spectacle at once so pathetic, so cruel, so shameful to the nations which permit it, as this migration of young girls lured by American industry.

Moral Self-education by Consumers

For nearly a quarter century the Consumers' League has been bringing to bear upon industry the intelligence of consumers in the interests of their own consciences and of the life, health, intelligence and well-being of wage workers. It has promoted short working hours for women and children, wage boards, and healthful conditions of work, and the abolition of child labor and of the sweating system. The League holds that consumers are entitled to a clean conscience if they act as conscientious people; that they can, if they will, enforce a claim to have all that they buy free from the taint of cruelty. By faithful organized inquiry they can ascertain the facts of industry, and when in the light of the facts standards are set up, consumers have power to enforce them. After this quarter century of modest experimental effort, it is clear that the enlightened consuming public is destined to play an increasing part in determining industrial morality.

Nothing could, however, be clearer than the teaching of this same quarter century's experience: that no one can, by individual effort alone, however patient and enlightened that effort may be, achieve any satisfying personal relation to industry. The larger the range and scope of the associated effort, the greater its value, particularly its educational value, for the participants. Thinking people are challenged to ceaseless effort to increase the enlightened power of consumers over production and distribution, by law, by publicity, by cooperation.

Our Preparation for the Change

Our lack is intellectual and spiritual. We distrust ourselves and each other. The mental energy of our ablest men has been too largely expended in industrial organization in the service of greed for dividends. We have been taught too long, and we have believed too credulously, that the profit motive is the best of which we are capable. The failure and crime that we see we attribute to the frailty of human nature, not, as the facts demand, to the corroding power of industry on a basis fundamentally immoral.

We all suffer a lack of moral sensitiveness because we are, throughout our lives, members of a society in which the average length of life of wage earners is conspicuously less than the life of prosperous people. We accept this with equanimity as we accept child labor, and avoidable night work even when performed by young girls, and the monstrous spectacle of wholesale poverty in the midst of riches beyond the power of the mind to compute or to conceive. Our industrial epoch has corroded our morals and hardened our hearts as surely as slavery injured its contemporaries, and far more subtly. There is grave reason to fear that it may have unfitted us for the oncoming stage of civilization, as slave owning unfitted the

white race for freedom and democracy, and left its
blight of race hatred from which the Republic still
suffers.

Acid tests of the industrial morality of every
public movement are the questions: "Does it tend
to restore to the people who work a share in the
ownership and control of the tools of industry?
Does it contribute to the ability of any group of
wage earners to fit themselves in mind, character
and economic position to participate helpfully in
the transition? Does it promote the enactment of
the industrial code?" Whatever is calculated to
enable us as a people, or any group among us, to
make a step forward on the road to peaceful service away from the battlefield of greed, is a contribution to the sum total of industrial morality.
And whatsoever hinders a forward step is in itself
actively evil, because it prolongs the existing evil.

We can retrieve our integrity only as we come
to accept as our ideal service instead of profit.
And this can be achieved only as industry becomes
a city, state, and national service. We are, indeed, confronted by the task of extending public
ownership of industry, and cooperative distribution of products, in the interest of the moral life
of the American people.

No one can predict how we, as a nation, shall
bear the strain of industry made collective, and

permanently a cooperative undertaking of citizens, without the relation of master and men. No prophet can foretell with certainty whether we can make that change peacefully, without a great revulsion and reaction, by reason of the uncooperative spirit in which we have all been bred. In the transition from the old industrial society we need to bring to bear all the wisdom, all the varied experience and discipline, that life has bestowed upon us all. We cannot safely omit from the common task any human soul however humble.

In each generation some cause arises which serves as a touchstone for the genuine democracy of mankind. Such to-day is the industrial transition. On the Pacific Coast and in the Northwest where the citizens have developed democratic institutions—the initiative, the referendum, the recall (including judges), equal suffrage, minimum wage boards, and the short working day—they go forward confidently with transition measures. There the conservation battle rages.

Indeed, the most hopeful feature of our outlook is our democracy, the fact that manhood suffrage has long been a matter of course in most of the states, the rapidly developing movement for giving votes to women, and the spread of the new devices of democracy eastward from the Pacific Coast.

It is the teachers' duty to prepare the minds of the next generation for carrying on the further stages of this industrial and political change. But how can the teachers themselves be fitted for their task?

The time of transition needs more than all things else socially minded people, multitudes of average men and women trained to habits of integrity and cooperation. But what preparation has been made for this?

Aside from building and loan associations, and farmers' clubs and other agricultural organizations, including the shippers' associations, we are almost without the experience of industrial cooperation.

Among industrial wage-earning people—outside the railway Brotherhoods—organization, associated action, has had to fight a losing battle for its life. In the steel industry, in the stock yards and packing houses, and in numerous other occupations there has been a systematic and largely successful movement to extinguish the unions, some of the most important of which have perished outright, while others have been permanently crippled.

The treasurer of a great manufacturing corporation explained to me with pride and pleasure some years ago, on the occasion of his leaving his office, that, in his opinion, his greatest service had consisted in the device which he had invented for making organization impossible among the employés. This device consisted in a rigid rule that, whenever the unskilled men in any department who spoke the same language reached the proportion of fifteen per cent. of all the men in that department, men speaking other languages must be engaged. This was avowedly for the purpose of making it difficult for the men to know each other. This method has since been widely adopted by large employers.

For five and twenty years the unions have been increasingly compelled to place themselves on a war footing, if they were to exist at all, and the enormous majority of wage earners are wholly unorganized. No preparation could be less adapted than this to a peaceful change to industry organized as a public service. Grave, indeed, is the responsibility of the men who have done this, gravest of all when, in the process, they have deprived working men and women of the constitutional rights of organization and assemblage, of freedom of speech and of the press!

The causal relation of industry to the present evils in social life and personal character has been slow to compel recognition, slower in this country than in Europe. With growing insight comes a challenge to our integrity of intellect and character. To see injustice without protesting is to share in it. To profit by recognized injustice is cynical.

This causal relation reveals itself naturally first to those who suffer acutely, to men and women who, working long and hard, get little pay, are injured in health, and die young. Their work brings them together in mines and mills, in industrial cities such as the world never before beheld, their daily experience is in common, they compare grievances, and are stimulated to common effort for the common good. Because they can achieve nothing alone, they are disciplined perforce to work together, to acquire whatever virtues come of voluntary association.

Just in proportion as they resist the inherent tendency of industry and participate in hastening the change they are agents of regeneration. Unlike the slaves who were set free without their own participation, unlike the coolies who were excluded without protest, the wage earners through their solidarity, their organizations, their political party, test the democracy of our time and are preparing, however haltingly, the conditions necessary to a higher and finer civilization.

The changed morality that is needed to make

the present transformation in our national life a
beneficent one is yet to be inculcated in the
schools, the colleges and universities. The teaching profession confronts to-day the noble task of
preparing the mind and spirit of the oncoming
generation for this change. Theirs is the new duty
of inculcating the new ideal of the democracy of
the future: the ideal of service performed not as
philanthropy, not as charity, not alone in the care
of childhood and old age, but in a transformed
industry, a universal service of men and women of
to-morrow—the direct, inevitable consequence of
the industrial development of to-day.

INDEX

141

For EU product safety concerns, contact us at Calle de José Abascal, 56–1°, 28003 Madrid, Spain or eugpsr@cambridge.org.

www.ingramcontent.com/pod-product-compliance
Ingram Content Group UK Ltd.
Pitfield, Milton Keynes, MK11 3LW, UK
UKHW012340130625
459647UK00009B/416